Journey Into the Mind of an

ISLAMIC TERRORIST

MARK A. GABRIEL, PhD

FRONT LINE
A Strang Company

Most Strang Communications/Charisma House/FrontLine/Siloam/Realms products are available at special quantity discounts for bulk purchase for sales promotions, premiums, fund-raising, and educational needs. For details, write Strang Communications/Charisma House/FrontLine/Siloam/Realms, 600 Rinehart Road, Lake Mary, Florida 32746, or telephone (407) 333-0600.

Journey Into the Mind of an Islamic Terrorist
by Mark A. Gabriel, PhD
Published by FrontLine
A Strang Company
600 Rinehart Road
Lake Mary, Florida 32746
www.strang.com

Unless otherwise noted, quotations from the Quran are from *The Noble Quran*, English Translation of the Meanings and Commentary published by King Fahd of Saudi Arabia in Medina, "The City of Light," Saudi Arabia in 1998. The translators were Dr. Muhammad Taqi-ud-Din al-Hilali and Dr. Muhammad Muhsin Khan.

Quotations from the Quran marked Ali translation are from *The Quran Translation*, 7th edition, by Abdullah Yusef Ali (Elmhurst, NY: Tahrike Tarsile Quran, Inc., 2001).

Quotations from the Quran marked Shakir Translation are from the electronically scanned versions of M. H. Shakir's English translation of the Holy Quran (Elmhurst, NY: Tahrike Tarsile Quran).

Editor's Note: Unless otherwise noted, all references to the book *The Armed Prophet* by Rifaat Sayed Ahmed, originally published in Arabic, were translated into the English language by Habib Srouji for Dr. Mark A. Gabriel (November 2004). Some electronic sources were translated from Arabic Web sites by the author. Whenever possible, source information is given in the Notes section.

Cover design by Karen Grindley

Library of Congress Cataloging-in-Publication Data

Gabriel, Mark A.
Journey into the mind of an Islamic terrorist / Mark Gabriel. -- 1st ed.
p. cm.
ISBN 1-59185-713-9 (pbk.)
1. Jihad. 2. Terrorism--Religious aspects--Islam. 3. Violence --Religious aspects--Islam. 4. Islamic fundamentalism. 5. Religion and politics--Islam. I. Title.
BP182.G34 2005
297.2'72--dc22
2005027225

First Edition

06 07 08 09 10 — 9 8 7 6 5 4 3 2 1
Printed in the United States of America

Dedicated to George W. Bush,
the president of the United States;
Tony Blair, the prime minister of Great Britain;
the American and British military;
the coalition in Iraq and Afghanistan;
the new Iraqi military that was born in the midst of the fire;
the CIA and the FBI;
the law enforcement agencies in the world's civilized countries
who are fighting together in the war against Islamic terrorism;
and the American and British people who are
standing behind their powerful leaders.

CONTENTS

PREFACE

This is my fourth book in five years on the topic of Islam, and my purpose for each one is to expose the facts about Islam to the Western reader. Over the course of these years, I have had an opportunity to see how people respond to my message. To be honest, at times I have been disappointed, particularly when people become belligerent and aggressive toward Muslims. So before you even begin reading, I would like to take the opportunity to challenge some misconceptions about my position.

First of all, I do not hate Muslims. I grew up as a Muslim in Egypt, and all of my family is still Muslim. (Incidentally, I no longer use my Muslim name in order to prevent radicals from harassing my family because of my writing.) I love the Muslim people. But I am not happy with the teachings of Islam because of the suffering they have caused the people of the Muslim world.

Here is my main point: people can learn to make a separation in their minds between the Muslim people and the teachings of Islam. A person can love and respect the Muslim people even if he rejects the teachings of Islam.

Second, I am not trying to say that all Muslims are radicals who secretly or openly want to kill every "infidel" (non-Muslim) they meet. That is ridiculous. The fact is that only a tiny percentage of Muslims are radical. All the other Muslims can be described as moderate, secular, traditional, or orthodox. They don't agree with the radicals at all. In fact, they are furious with them for making their lives difficult.

Third, having knowledge about Islam does not give anyone permission to insult Muslims. The purpose of my writing is not to make you hate Muslims, but to arm you with information about Islam so that as a citizen you can support the best course of action to protect your society.

Fourth, I do not want to vilify or dehumanize the Islamic radicals in your eyes. On the contrary, I hope you can see them as unique human beings whose defining characteristic is a desire to be true to the teachings of Islam. They are dangerous now, but they were not born evil. Perhaps this is easy for me to remember because I grew up as a Muslim in Egypt during the 1960s and 1970s. Everyone my age knew of a friend or relative who joined a radical group and, as a result, ruined his life.

Finally, I want to say thank you for picking up this book. Not many people take the time to find out the truth about Islam for themselves. They would rather spend thirty minutes watching someone on television tell them what to think. By reading this book, you will be able to look at the facts and draw your own conclusions. People like you make up a small percentage of society, but you will make a great impact. By understanding the mind of the Islamic terrorist, you will be able to support public policy that will stop their violence.

And there is another way you can help to stop the violence also. I believe that this book is an excellent support tool for all public officials involved in anti-terrorist work. I recommend that you give a copy of this book to your local law enforcement officers—sheriffs, policemen, local security officers involved in anti-terrorism work, and so on. You may even want to present a copy to some of your local government officials as your thank you for their work in keeping you and your family safe from the violence of terrorism.

INTRODUCTION

Many excellent writers can tell you in great detail about who, what, where, when, and how Islamic radicals are operating all around the world. They can describe political and economic conditions that are helping to create more radicals, but they often fall short of explaining the radicals' motives. In other words, you have received a lot of information about *what* radicals are doing. I am going to answer the question many westerners have asked: *Why* are they doing this?

I am going to answer that question from the point of view of a "religious radical." In other words, I acknowledge that radicals and terrorists also have political, economic, social, or psychological motives, but I am going to focus on the religious motive, which is the most powerful and the most dangerous factor. It is also the most ignored and misunderstood factor in the world media, so I believe I can make a useful contribution by focusing on it.

To journey inside the mind of a religious radical, we can read what the radical writers have left for us. Writings by some authors, such as Sayyid Qutb or Abul ala Mawdudi, are easily available in English. But other writings are still only available in Arabic, and even then they can be difficult to find. Sometimes academic people read them and discuss them, but the information rarely is packaged in a form that the public can use. In fact, most Arabic-speaking people have not seen these documents either.

My analysis of radical philosophy draws heavily from these hard-to-find documents. I think this book's most important contribution to the public debate is allowing more people to see the source material of radical thought.

I want you to have a deep understanding of radical thinking; therefore, this book gives you more than just a summary of their writings.

I describe the modern roots of Islamic radicalism and the backgrounds of the key writers before I describe their writings. Afterward, I show you the source of their philosophy by telling you how Muhammad practiced jihad, drawing from my doctorate degree in Islamic history and culture from Al-Azhar University in Cairo. Finally, the book ends on a note of hope because I believe there are ways to control radicalism and restore peace between Islam and the rest of the world.

The book is divided into the following sections:

Section 1: A Wall Between Brothers

To give you an idea of my perspective on this topic, I will tell you a little information about my personal experiences with radical Islamic philosophy. My best friend from childhood became a member of the most dangerous radical group in Egypt at the time, and the tragedy of his life is a microcosm of the havoc that these groups cause.

Section 2: The Islamic Great Awakening

This section tells the personal stories of the radical writers during the rise of modern Islamic fundamentalism. It moves through three generations of leaders described as the Founders, the Evangelists, and the Prisoners, and concludes with the Aristocrats, who are Osama bin Laden and Ayman al-Zawahiri. You will also learn how Ayman al-Zawahiri, second in command of Al-Qaeda, uses Muhammad's example to justify suicide bombing.

Section 3: Five Pillars of Radical Philosophy

This section synthesizes radical writings into the key concepts that motivate their activity. I have identified those themes and present them to you as the "five pillars of radical philosophy." This material is original and unique to my book.

Section 4: Warning About Deceit

World leaders need to know that Muhammad taught that deceit is a powerful strategy of war. This section quotes his specific teaching and explains how deceit is practiced today. It also includes an entire chapter on al-Zawahiri's specific teaching about deceit, which I downloaded from radical Web sites in Arabic.

Section 5: Following Muhammad's Footsteps

History is relived in the present, and this section reviews Muhammad's use of jihad and how his example has been followed by Muslim leaders until the present time.

Section 6: Hope for the Future

At some point as you read this book you might be tempted to think, *This is hopeless.* If you only look at the present, you can feel this way. But there are signs of hope coming from Egypt and the Middle East. For example, the grandfather of all radical groups, the Muslim Brotherhood, adopted a policy of nonviolence after Egyptian President Sadat released many of them from prison. Al-Gama'a al-Islamiyyah, which led a bloody campaign against the Egyptian government for more than fifteen years, declared a cease-fire in 1997. Based on this recent history, this section explores a two-pronged approach to stopping Islamic terrorism.

Conclusion

Though Islamic radicals may be successful at spreading terror today, they have no chance at all of winning against a world united against them. The great challenge is strategy. The purpose of this book is to provide information that will help create the best strategy.

SECTION 1
A WALL BETWEEN BROTHERS

1

MY BEST FRIEND KAMAL

A lot of times our image of an Islamic radical is what we see on television—cruel, legalistic, malevolent. When a man videotapes himself cutting off someone else's head with a knife, indeed a line of decency has been crossed. Yet, there was a time for every one of these people when they were not radical terrorists. They were typical members of society—high school or university students, doctors, businessmen, teachers, or religious leaders.

Why did they choose to cross the line?

To help you understand the answer to that question, I want to take you back to my childhood and tell you about my best friend, Kamal.*

Growing Up Together

Kamal and I were classic childhood friends, growing up together in a middle-class Muslim neighborhood in Egypt. In the mornings we trudged to school together, and in the afternoons we gleefully ran home. We faithfully went to the same neighborhood mosque for five prayers a day at approximately 4:00 a.m., 12:00 p.m., 3:00 p.m., 5:00 p.m., and 8:30 p.m. (Prayer times are based on the time of sunrise, so they vary according to the season.)

After the third prayer of the day, we had free time to grab our fishing poles to fish in the River Nile or to go swimming in the river on hot days. When we had a big group of boys together, we played soccer.

*This is not my friend's real name. I chose to use a pseudonym to protect his family's privacy.

There was only one major difference between Kamal and me: my parents sent me to a religious primary school sponsored by Al-Azhar* while my friend attended public school provided by the Egyptian government.

We learned similar things, but I received a lot of additional teaching about the Quran and the life of Muhammad. My religious training was intense: the goal was to memorize the entire Quran, which is about the length of the New Testament. Every day my class would recite for our teachers the new verses we had learned.

Kamal always asked me about what I learned, and I always loved to tell him. He was a great friend.

War Leader Against Christians

My religious education, however, had a terrible effect on my attitude toward Christians. My teachers told me, "Christians hate you. They want to wipe Islam off the face of the earth. The Quran tells us exactly that they will never be our friends unless we covert to Christianity. 'O you who believe! take not the Jews and the Christians for your friends and protectors: they are but friends and protectors to each other'" (Surah 5:51, Ali translation).

In Egypt during the 1960s, neighborhoods were segregated according to Christian or Muslim. I, of course, lived in a Muslim neighborhood, but across the canal from our neighborhood was a Christian neighborhood.

When we were about ten or eleven years old, Kamal and I decided that these Christians needed to learn a lesson from us (Muslims). We got a group of boys together and said, "We are starting a war against the Christians." Each of us put on the white robe with long sleeves that we wore to go to the mosque (called a *gallibiyah*). Then we lifted up the front of the robe to make a big pocket and filled it full of stones.

We must have been quite a sight—fifteen skinny boys marching down the street with our robes full of stones, kicking up clouds of dust as we went. Our hearts were pounding as we crossed the bridge over the canal to the Christian neighborhood. "Let's go!" I shouted.

We ran into the neighborhood, picked a target house, and started

*Al-Azhar is the most powerful school in the Islamic world. It has up to ninety thousand students on campuses throughout Egypt.

throwing rocks. I heard glass shattering as the stones met their marks.

Soon, the front doors opened and people started yelling, "Stop! What are you doing?" We scattered away, back over the bridge to the other side of the canal—the Muslim side.

You would think that this would be the first and last time we did this prank. But the Christians of Egypt lived in fear and submission to Muslims. Not one family called the police or even complained to my family about what we did. Kamal and I did "war on the Christians" many times.

Looking back, I can see that while I was just a little child, my religious training planted seeds of hatred in my heart. I believed what my teachers told me about non-Muslims and took the next logical step. However, my parents did not believe in attacking non-Muslims. When my father finally found out what we were doing to the Christians, he beat me with a rope. But it didn't change my heart. I was just angrier.

A Wedge Between Us

As Kamal and I went through middle school, we remained the best of friends. I finished memorizing the Quran at the age of twelve, which was a tremendous accomplishment and earned me great respect in the Muslim community. My family threw a big party to celebrate, and Kamal was there with me. By high school I was qualified to lead prayers at our neighborhood mosque. When I had my chance to lead the prayers at the mosque, I could look out and see my friend Kamal in the rows of worshipers. Our friendship was still strong, but two things happened to change that.

First, I played a prank on a Christian monk that nearly killed him. While the monk was riding past our house on his donkey, I slipped a small, homemade bomb in the saddlebag. When it exploded, the donkey reared up and the monk fell off and hit his head on the ground. He was in the hospital for months. But when he got out, he came to meet with me at my parents' house. All he said to me was, "I forgive you." After that day, I could not hold on to my hatred against Christians. Kamal, however, never agreed with my change of heart.

Second, a new group began recruiting at Kamal's high school, calling students to a higher level of commitment to Islam. It was Al-Gama'a al-Islamiyyah, the radical group that later assassinated Egyptian President Anwar Sadat and murdered thousands of other people in an attempt to take over the Egyptian government.

Kamal was fascinated by their accounts of how the first Muslims lived together and fought for Islam. They told great stories about heroes of the faith, like Khalid ibn Walid, a man so effective in battle he became known as the "Sword of Allah." Al-Gama'a al-Islamiyyah painted a much idealized picture of early Islam, and it was inspiring. Students wanted to bring those days back. They wanted to practice Islam that way in their daily lives.

Kamal was also impressed with how Al-Gama'a practiced social justice on the high school campus. They would provide books, clothing, and monthly support to poor students. Kamal grew up in a comfortable, middle-class family. He didn't need the support. But he saw Al-Gama'a helping students who were not being helped by the secular government.

Al-Gama'a did not hide their belief in the sword of Islam. For example, the high school students often sang this song:

I Shall Avenge My God and Belief

I shall avenge my God and belief
And go by my religion in full confidence
To achieve victory above all people
Or to God I go, dwelling eternally.
We carry the sword, lions of honor,
Delivering a taste of death and hell to the unbelievers.

Imagine a group of high school boys singing about "delivering death and hell to the unbelievers."

Another way Al-Gama'a solidified its recruits was to take them on retreats outside of town. The boys camped and played soccer, but they also learned the philosophy of Al-Gama'a. Kamal went on his first retreat during the first year of high school. He came back ready to recruit everyone for Al-Gama'a, but I refused to join him.

I didn't like the way they dressed and let their beards grow. I didn't like the way they tried to use classical Arabic words to talk to each other and how they tried to copy Muhammad's way of eating food. Specifically, since Muhammad had no fork and spoon, they would not use a fork and spoon. They ate with their hands—in fact, with only their thumb and two fingers because that is how Islamic history records that Muhammad ate.

I also felt they were walking on a path where they couldn't see the end. To me there was nothing but a dangerous end. They would harm others and harm themselves. I told my friend, "These people are poor in learning Islam. You can't believe everything they say." Kamal was upset with me.

By his second year of high school, Kamal was leading the Al-Gama'a's student retreat. He was a different person now, very critical of all those around him. He tried to stop his sisters from watching TV, and he wanted his oldest sister to cover her hair. He was so judgmental that he turned their family life into a living hell. His father couldn't believe it—his oldest son—turning on them. His mother's heart was broken.

By his third year of high school, Kamal stopped going to our neighborhood mosque. He said it was a secular mosque, not practicing Islam. He went to a mosque where the Al-Gama'a people went, about four miles away. We stopped seeing each other. I felt hurt because I saw that he was walking on a dangerous road and did not care about his family or our friendship.

Rising Stars

When Kamal graduated from high school, we all knew he would go to college because he was very bright, particularly in math. His family expected him to study mechanical engineering or civil engineering. They were quite surprised when he chose to study chemical engineering at an institute in southern Egypt.

For my part, I chose to continue religious studies, and with the full support of my family I went to Al-Azhar University in Cairo to study Islamic history and culture.

Kamal climbed the ranks of leadership in Al-Gama'a while he was in college. To raise money for Al-Gama'a, Kamal led attacks against Christian pharmacies in southern Egypt, robbing the shops and often killing the owners. It broke my heart to hear what he was doing.

We didn't see each other until 1981 when Al-Gama'a arranged for a nationwide retreat at the Grand Mosque of Al-Azhar, where I was still a student. Since the retreat was in the mosque where Al-Azhar students went to pray, I couldn't avoid it.

The Al-Gama'a members had taken up residence in the mosque. During the day, they were soaking in lectures from Ayman al-Zawahiri, who is now the No. 2 man in Al-Qaeda. They slept on the floor at night.

During this retreat, I walked into the mosque for prayer and came face-to-face with Kamal. We talked a few minutes, but it wasn't long before we were arguing.

"You're a fool," I mocked him.

"You're an infidel," he retorted.

"Who gave you the right to decide who is Muslim and who is an infidel?" I argued.

"Go read the Quran," he challenged.

"I have," I spat back.

"There will be a day," he growled, "when we are going to take over Al-Azhar."

I had no idea that before the year would end, Al-Gama'a would assassinate Egyptian President Sadat as they attempted to take over the government and create an Islamic state. Most of the group's members were captured and thrown in prison, including Kamal. He spent a year in federal prison.

I don't know exactly what the guards did to him in prison, but it is very likely that he was tortured. He came out a broken person. He rejected radicalism, but at the same time he didn't know how to carry on.

Years later, our hearts and minds would be together again, but I will not tell that chapter of the story now. For now let me simply say that Kamal found peace before his life ended at the young age of thirty-eight. It's a sad story that I will tell at the end of this book.

Broken Lives

So when I write about radical Muslims, I know they can be cruel, bloodthirsty killers, and I hate what they do. But at the same time, I remember that each one started out as a little boy, just like my friend Kamal or me. And for all the "successful" terrorists that we see on the news, there are many more broken human beings who realize that they have taken the wrong path and don't know how to find their way back.

Radical Islam stole Kamal away from his family and his friends. But that is just a tiny picture of what was happening all over Egypt as a revival of Islamic fundamentalism swept the nation and the Muslim world. Traditional Muslims, like me, were forced to look at their faith and ask, "What do we really believe?"

2

GRASSROOTS RADICALISM IN EGYPT

The voices of my father, mother, and sister pulled me awake from my noon nap on a hot day in October 1981. They were talking loudly and excitedly, and I could hear the sound of the television in the background. I hurried out into the family room and asked, "What is going on?"

"We aren't sure," my father told me. "There's been a shooting during the military parade. The television says that the president has been injured and that he is in the hospital." Confusion immediately gripped the country. We all went into the street to talk to the neighbors about what had happened. Soon, the news stopped broadcasting, and the government television and radio stations played nothing but a man reciting the Quran. That's when we all suspected that Sadat was probably dead.

All over the world, news media were broadcasting that Sadat had been assassinated, but the people of Egypt were the last to know when the news was officially broadcast in the country that evening. At the same time, Vice President Hosni Mubarek declared martial law.

At first, many of us thought that the military had tried to take over the country because the shots came from a soldier participating in the parade. Others thought Mubarek had orchestrated it all. It was similar to the first days after 9/11 when the people of the United States were trying to figure out who had attacked them. After two days we finally learned that the attack had been orchestrated by Al-Jihad, an Islamic radical group.

Mubarek launched a ruthless campaign to eliminate radicals from Egypt. I focused on my studies and avoided radicals as much as possible.

But their philosophy was sweeping Egypt like wildfire, and I wanted to find out how they convinced people like my friend Kamal to join them. My opportunity came in a place I least expected it.

The Power of the Abandoned Duty

I finished my bachelor's degree in 1984, and in 1985 I started my mandatory service time in the Egyptian army. When I was assigned to my duty at my military unit, there was one major who was especially glad to see me. He was the second in command, and he had been leading the prayers five times a day at the base because there was no one else qualified to do it. I had been qualified to lead prayers since I was in high school, and he happily turned that duty over to me.

So I began to lead the prayers and to preach on Fridays. However, the first time he heard me preach, he was concerned about my theology. I was preaching the Islam of cooperation and kindness. But this major's father was a member of the Muslim Brotherhood (a large radical group founded in Egypt), and he believed in the call of jihad.

He was surprised that I, a scholar who had studied Islam deeply, would not agree with him. We began to debate, and during the course of our discussions he brought me a manuscript to read to support his case. It was a photocopy of a thin book titled *The Abandoned Duty*, written by Abdul Salam Faraj. This book was officially illegal, but copies were being passed from hand to hand around the country.

"Look," the army major told me, "Faraj was an engineer, not an Islamic scholar, but even he could understand the meaning of jihad."

I took the book and read it privately. I had to be careful because if the police caught me, they would take the book and interrogate me. Because I was known to be moderate, I could tell them I was reading the book for research, and I would be fine. But if I was forced to tell them that I got the book from a superior officer in the army, the major would have been in trouble because he had a known connection with the Muslim Brotherhood (through his father), and he was distributing illegal materials to the lower ranks. Mubarek would throw him into jail, and there is no telling what would happen to him there.

No one caught me with the book. After I read it, I returned it to the major, and we continued to debate. The author (Faraj) was a product of the revival of Islamic fundamentalism that swept through the different schools and universities around Egypt. Only twenty-seven years old when he wrote the book, he passionately and persuasively called for the young people of his generation to fulfill the abandoned duty of jihad and fight the secular government of Egypt. He also quoted many Islamic scholars for support, especially the highly respected medieval scholar Ibn Taymiyyah. Faraj had been executed by the Egyptian government for his role in the assassination of President Anwar Sadat three years earlier, so now he was a martyr and a hero. There was little I could do to change the major's mind.

Just a few months later in March 1986, my required time in the military was finished. I went back to Al-Azhar University to start working on my master's degree. I never imagined that someday I would write a book about the mind-set of Islamic radicals and I would again see Faraj's words.

An Interesting Thing Happened in History Class

At Al-Azhar University I was studying to earn a master's degree in Islamic history and culture. This was a dangerous thing to do. Why? Because students of Islamic history often experience one of two powerful reactions to what they have learned.

First, Muslim history students often end up with serious doubts about their faith. I have known many Muslims who have experienced this. About forty years ago, the Great Imam of Al-Azhar recognized this and considered outlawing the study of Islamic history at Al-Azhar altogether!

I experienced this effect personally. In my studies, I saw how the teachings of Islam produced a history that was a bloodbath from beginning to present. Even the first four leaders after Muhammad's death were focused on fighting and war. In my last year at Al-Azhar, I began to openly question whether some who were considered heroes of the faith should be condemned as criminals instead.

In the Islamic world, it is utterly unacceptable to judge history this way. If I had stayed in Egypt, I would not be a free man today. I would either be dead or in jail.

Second, a Muslim history student may have the opposite reaction and choose to take history as a guide for his personal life. This person becomes a radical. The powerful leaders of Islamic radicalism are not desperate, poor youths with no hope for the future. They are well-educated men who have studied Islam deeply. Some of the top modern leaders have memorized the entire Quran, including Ayatollah Khomeini and Sheikh Omar Abdul Rahman.

The Constitution of Al-Jihad

In 1990, I succeeded in graduating from Al-Azhar with a doctorate degree, keeping my doubts to myself. Al-Azhar hired me as a lecturer, and I also became the imam of a small mosque. The year was 1992, when Al-Gama'a had launched a new, bloody offensive against the Egyptian government.

At the mosque one day after prayer, one of the high school students came to me and said, "May I ask you a question?"

"Of course, my brother," I answered.

"Someone at my school gave me a copy of the *Constitution of Al-Jihad*," he said in a hushed voice. "Are these people speaking the truth?" He looked at me earnestly.

My blood boiled inside me as I heard these words. I thought, *How dare these people continue to prey on high school students!* Al-Jihad was the military branch of Al-Gama'a al-Islamiyyah, the group my friend Kamal had joined. Ayman al-Zawahiri and Sheikh Abdul Rahman led Al-Gama'a at this time. This group was waging war against the Egyptian government, killing police, secret agents, Christians, tourists, and even Egyptian Muslims. But outwardly I stayed calm and answered, "My brother, please bring me this book. I would like to read it."

He did what I asked and later brought me a faded photocopy of a handwritten document. It was called a "constitution" because the popular saying of the time was, "The Quran is our constitution, and the prophet is our leader." While sitting in Egyptian prison cells, three notorious leaders of Al-Jihad had handwritten these pages: Abod Zoummar, Karam Zohdy, and Assim Abdul Majed. Bit by bit the pages were smuggled out of prison. By 1987, photocopies were being circulated throughout Egypt. Like Faraj's book, it was illegal to have a copy.

The boy told me, "Please give it back to me when you are done because the man who gave it to me said I need to return it to him."

I took it home with me and read it in one day. I quickly saw that the purpose of the book was to justify the assassination of Sadat and to call for continued war against the "secular" government of Egypt.

The powerful use of Arabic language combined with quotes from the Quran and Islamic scholars was like pouring gasoline on a fire. This was dangerous material!

At that time I believed that the fundamentalists were all wrong about the message of Islam. How could the real God demand that His followers kill their fellow countrymen in the name of faith? I always took the peaceful side of Islam, the side that lets you get along with other people, so I wanted to protect this good young man from this philosophy. I warned him, "Get away from these people. Don't be in touch with them." I could just see him following the path my friend Kamal took. I didn't want to see him start killing others in the name of Allah.

"What about the photocopy of the book?" he asked. He was worried about returning it.

"You don't need to return it," I said. There was no way I was going to let it get into another teenager's hands.

When I preached at the mosque on Friday, I challenged the people to question the tactics of these radical groups, "What Islam are these groups talking about, where you kill my brother, my neighbor, the policeman just working to feed his kids—why do you kill these innocent people? This is jihad?"

But my words were not being received. People accused me of not being a committed Muslim and only teaching the Islam that the government wanted me to teach.

Inner Conflict

What they didn't realize was that inside I too was questioning my understanding of Islam. The arguments in the *Constitution of Al-Jihad* were not based on lies—they were based on the facts in the Quran and the sunnah (the life of Muhammad). As one who had memorized the entire Quran as well as several thousand hadith, I could not argue with their facts. This led me to a new line of questioning—a question of the truth.

What if the Islamic radicals were truly the ones who followed the teachings of Islam? What did that say about Islam? Was this what the true God would require of His people?

As I was struggling with these questions, I continued my duties as imam and also as a teacher at Al-Azhar University, but I asked too many questions. About two months after I read the manuscript, I was called before the university committee for policy enforcement. They wanted to see where I stood with my faith. I finally told them, "We say the Quran is directly from Allah, but I doubt it. I see in it the thoughts of a man, not of the one true God."

One professor jumped up and starting cursing me. By the end of the meeting, I was fired. The next morning the secret police came with machine guns, kidnapped me from my house, and threw me into prison for interrogation (where I was tortured). They suspected that I had converted to Christianity, and they wanted to find out who had led me astray.

Islamic Jihad in a New Light

You can read the details about my time in prison in my previous books. Let me say that I tasted only a small bit of the torture that other prisoners have felt in Egyptian prisons. For example, my friend Kamal was in prison for a year. I was only there for two weeks.

After a person is tortured in Egyptian prison, he will come out either questioning what he believes or dangerously hardened against the governmental powers. I came out of prison emotionally shaken and thoroughly disgusted with how Islam was being practiced. I wanted nothing to do with Islam any longer. What I wanted to find was the true God of heaven.

After a year, I found myself reading the New Testament of the Bible for the first time. I saw the words of Matthew 5:38–39:

> You have heard that it was said, "Eye for eye, and tooth for tooth." But I tell you, Do not resist an evil person. If someone strikes you on the right cheek, turn to him the other also.

My whole body began trembling as I saw in these words the heart of the God of heaven. They were truth. With no persuasion from any Christian, monk, or missionary, I said in my heart, *I follow Jesus Christ.*

As I read more of the Bible in the weeks that followed, I remembered my copy of the *Constitution of Al-Jihad.* (I had kept it hidden in my room all this time.) My mind was exploding with the differences between these two philosophies. With my background in academics, I did what came naturally: I put the two manuscripts side by side and wrote a book about them.

At the time, I was being mentored by monks at an Egyptian church. I gave them my copy of the *Constitution of Al-Jihad* and the book I had written about it. I wanted to let them see the kind of philosophy that was circulating around the country.

Less than a year later (in 1994) I was forced to leave Egypt permanently, and I left the manuscript behind. I assumed that was the last time I would ever see a copy of the *Constitution of Al-Jihad.*

My Second Chance

It's been a little more than ten years since I left Egypt. I spent six years in South Africa before coming to the United States in 2000. The following year, the 9/11 attacks took place, and I wrote my first book in America titled *Islam and Terrorism.* The following year I wrote *Islam and the Jews* to help westerners understand the traditional Islamic position toward Israel. In 2004 I finished a book titled *Jesus and Muhammad,* which used the original sources of Islam and Christianity to compare the two most influential men of all history.

When I wrote my first book, I had real difficulty getting access to the classical Islamic sources for hadith, biography of the prophet, and history. But by the time I wrote *Jesus and Muhammad,* my editor could search in English, online, for specific words in hadith! The explosion of information is amazing. Yet I never expected what I found when I started research for the book you are holding in your hands now.

Two years ago I heard about an Arabic book titled *The Armed Prophet.* It was written by Rifaat Sayed Ahmed, an expert in political science in the Egyptian National Research Center for Society and Crime (an Egyptian government agency). It was an academic book describing the rise of radicalism in Egypt. But what excited me is that *The Armed Prophet* included, in their entirety, the two manuscripts that I had read in Egypt—the *Constitution of Al-Jihad* and *The Abandoned Duty* by Abdul Salam Faraj!

I knew I had to buy the book. I tried to get it online from the publisher, but then I found out that I could buy it at a bookstore in Virginia. No hassles—just walk in and buy it. I will never cease to be amazed at the literature I can buy in a free country. I assure you that the other people who are buying this book are radicals, not researchers.

Now I had a second chance to do what I had started in Egypt—expose the mind-set of the Muslim radical.

Beginning the Journey

Let's begin our journey into the mind of the Islamic radical. First, we need to get to know these people as human beings, so the next section of the book will describe the lives of the most influetial modern radical leaders.

Remember, we are going to focus on the key writers/philosophers of the movement because their ideas are feeding the radicals of today. These writers can be divided into four groups.

1. The Founders

These men were scholars of Islam, and through great organization skills and deeply inspirational writing, they spread a return to Islamic fundamentalism starting in the late 1920s. Their call for jihad was clear but sophisticated. Many conservative Muslim Web sites make their writings available in Arabic, English, and other languages. The names to know are: Hasan al-Banna, Sayyid Abul ala Mawdudi, and Sayyid Qutb.

2. The Evangelists

These men took the writings of the founders to heart and gave their lives to put them into practice during the 1970s and 1980s. The life cycle of these writers was to become committed to radical Islam, found their own radical group, write a manifesto of their position, carry out an attack against the government, get captured, go on trial, and be executed. These writings are rarely available in English or analyzed in depth, but they are fueling the next generation of radicals. The names to know are Dr. Salah Sariah, Shokri Mustafa, and Abdul Salam Faraj.

3. The Prisoners

This group is different from the evangelists because they were not executed for their attacks against the government. Instead, they were kept in prison, where they wrote two manuscripts in the 1980s defending their jihad against Egyptian authority. The names to know are Abod Zoummar, Karam Zohdy, and Assim Abdul Maghed.

4. The Aristocrats

In the late 1980s, two new leaders became prominent in radical Islam. Unlike their predecessors, they were men of privilege and means. After successfully pushing the Soviet Union out of Afghanistan, they turned their sites toward a new target and masterminded the attacks of 9/11. The names to know are Osama bin Laden and Ayman al-Zawahiri.

As you read about each group of men in the next section, you will learn what personal and political factors pushed them to become radicals. This information will prepare you to understand the analysis of their writings that comes in Section 3.

SECTION 2
THE ISLAMIC GREAT AWAKENING

THE FOUNDERS

	Hasan al-Banna	Abul ala Mawdudi	Sayyid Qutb
Birth/death	1906–1949	1903–1979	1906–1965
Nationality	Egyptian	Indian	Egyptian
Education	Studied to be an elementary school Arabic language teacher; memorized the Quran by age 10.	Religious education focused on Islamic languages—Arabic and Farsi. His native language is Urdu.	Religious education at Al-Azhar; memorized Quran by age 10.
Name of group	Founder of the Muslim Brotherhood, the first modern Muslim radical group, 1928	Founder of Jema'at e-Islami, 1941	Member of the Muslim Brotherhood, 1950
Key Publications	*Al Aqaa'id* [The Principles], *Our Message*	150 books, including *Understanding the Quran, Toward Understanding Islam, Let Us Be Muslims*	*Milestones Along the Road* (1964, written from prison) and others
Crimes	Assassinations of enemies of the Muslim Brotherhood, culminating in the assassination of Egyptian Prime Minister Nuqrashi Pasha, 1949	Leading rebellion against secular leaders of Pakistan in order to establish Islamic government	Attempted overthrow of Egyptian government; author of *Milestones Along the Road*
Type of death	Assassination, presumably by Egyptian secret service, 1949	Old age	Execution by Egyptian government, 1965
Age at death	43	76	59
Status of group today	Still working to establish Islamic government and law, but have abandoned violence and use preaching and politics instead.	Supported the Taliban in Afghanistan, Osama bin Laden and Al-Qaeda. Killed journalist Daniel Pearl.	Still working to establish Islamic government and law, but have abandoned violence and use preaching and politics instead.

3
THE FOUNDERS

During the 1970s young people in the United States began to question themselves and society as U.S. troops fought an unpopular war in Vietnam. The Christian community faced a time of questioning as well. Various movements conscientiously tried to return to the principles of the Bible as opposed to the traditions of the church. The Charismatic Renewal shook up churches by encouraging people to take action and experience their faith rather than just talk about it.

Something similar was happening in the Islamic world in the 1960s and 1970s. The Islamic world was like a house fallen into disrepair, and Muslims were asking themselves why. In 1924 they had lost the caliphate, the seat of authority that had united Muslim nations. Muslim lands in the Middle East went through a period of being controlled by European colonial powers, starting with Napoleon's invasion of Egypt in 1798. Though independence was restored to most of them between the 1950s and the 1970s, corrupt governments oppressed the Middle East nations, and the common people lived in poverty. They were lagging behind the rest of the world in development and technology. Western morals and values were seeping into society, to the dismay of traditional Muslims.

Muslims began to say, "Our problem is that we have left our faith. If we lived according to the Quran and the sunnah, our world would be perfect. We could bring back the glory days of Islam." Just as Christians wanted to return to the teachings of the Bible, the Muslim revivalists wanted to return to the teachings of the Quran and the sunnah (the words and actions of the prophet Muhammad). They cried out against academic study of Islam and demanded that Islam be put into action. This "great awakening of Islam" affected the entire Islamic world.

To borrow a term from Christian history, we could say that Islam experienced a fundamentalist revival. According to Webster's dictionary, Christian *fundamentalism* emphasizes "the literally interpreted Bible as fundamental to Christian life and teaching." In the same way, Islamic fundamentalism emphasizes the literally interpreted Quran and sunnah as fundamental to Muslim life and teaching.

Islamic fundamentalism became a powerful movement through the leadership of a twenty-one-year-old college graduate who had just started his first job as an Arabic language teacher at a primary school in Egypt. His name was Hasan al-Banna. This is one of the most famous names in the entire Islamic world. Let's see what took him from being a schoolteacher to becoming known as the grandfather of modern Islamic terrorism.

Hasan al-Banna Spreads the Great Awakening

Born in 1906, Hasan al-Banna was a precocious and devout child. He finished memorizing the Quran around age ten, which is a very early age. Even in elementary school he joined several religious societies that promoted Islamic morals. He started practicing Muslim evangelism and preaching when he was twelve years old.[1]

Hasan al-Banna's father was a watch repairman, but he also had an Al-Azhar education and served as prayer leader and Quranic teacher at the local mosque. He was a specialist in the science of hadith and wrote a famous book called *Al Fath Al Rabany* [Divine Invasion and Conquest]. He instilled strong religious values in al-Banna.

Ever precocious, at the age of thirteen, Hasan al-Banna fought in the Egyptian revolution against the British (1919). At the age of sixteen he went to Cairo University and graduated four years later. While he was at the university, the Muslim caliphate collapsed, and he saw with dismay that secular, Western ways had penetrated the Muslim society. After graduation in 1927, he went to work in the city of Ismailiyya as an Arabic language teacher at an elementary school and as a preacher and teacher in mosques. He became the most popular teacher in the city and evangelized people everywhere—coffee shops, parks, public transportation, and in the streets.

In 1928, he, his brother, and four friends gathered at his house and swore to live and die for Islam. The Muslim Brotherhood was born. At first, they were just another one of the many small Islamic groups of that time. But Hasan al-Banna had a great gift of organization, and his group grew dramatically. By 1932, he had moved the headquarters of his movement to Cairo and became very active, traveling all over Egypt. By the end of the decade he had established branches in every Egyptian province. By the end of the 1940s, in Egypt alone the Muslim Brotherhood had 500,000 active members and an equal number of sympathizers. The Muslim Brotherhood set up numerous schools, mosques, and factories.[2]

The Muslim Brotherhood started out as a movement for spiritual and moral reform, but as it grew, it began to put pressure on Egyptian politics as well. The Muslim Brotherhood tried to assassinate Egyptian Prime Minister Nuqrashi Pasha, and as a result, in 1948 the Egyptian government voted to make the Muslim Brotherhood illegal in Egypt and arrested many members. Less than three weeks later, a Brotherhood member succeeded in assassinating the prime minister.

In 1949, just a month later, Hasan al-Banna was shot on a street in Cairo. Members of the movement later claimed that the Egyptian government killed him after he arrived at the hospital. Current conventional wisdom says the assassination was carried out by the Egyptian secret police. The Egyptian government prohibited a funeral procession. Only immediate family members went behind the body to the cemetery.

The Muslim Brotherhood was not the same without its charismatic leader, but it certainly survived and is still active today. It was up to two great writers to carry on al-Banna's message and fuel the Islamic Great Awakening.

Fueling the Fires of Revival

The two great writers were Abul ala Mawdudi (considered the father of the Muslim radical movement in Asia) and Sayyid Qutb[3] (referred to as the Martin Luther of the radical movement in the Middle East). Their writings are still widely read today, and they can be found on many Web sites in Arabic and English. Because their place in history was intertwined, I examined their lives in parallel and was surprised by the similarities.

Education

Mawdudi was born in 1903 in South India, and Qutb was born in 1906 in a village in the Asyut province of Egypt. When they were young, both children were given a religious education by their parents. This training would influence them for the rest of their lives.

Mawdudi

Mawdudi's father studied Islamic law at one of the largest Islamic universities in Asia, and he worked as a teacher and lawyer. He taught his son about Islamic law, the Quran, and the history of Islam, especially in Asia. When he was eleven, Mawdudi's father sent him to an Islamic school where he focused on learning language, particularly Arabic (the language of the Quran) and Farsi, the Persian language. (His mother tongue was Urdu.) Mawdudi was an extremely gifted child, and he graduated with a bachelor's degree by the age of fifteen.

Mawdudi left his hometown at the age of fifteen and went to work as a newspaper editor in Baghnoor. After a little while, the British authority in India closed down the newspaper. It was the year 1919, and the Islamic caliphate in Turkey had reached a dangerous stage of weakness. Mawdudi joined a new movement in India aimed at reviving the caliphate. Although he was busy with the problems in India, he also set his sights on revival all over the Islamic world. His writing became famous in many Muslim countries. One of his most famous books was titled *Jihad in Islam,* which he completed in 1928, four years after the collapse of the caliphate when he was a young man of twenty-five.

Qutb

When Qutb was young, his father and mother had a disagreement about his education. Qutb's mother wanted him to go to the government public school while his father wanted him to go to an Al-Azhar primary school. In the beginning, his mother won out and he went to public school—but only for a short while. Then his father put him in an Al-Azhar elementary school, and Qutb excelled. He finished memorizing the entire Quran at the age of ten, which is a very young age to finish memorizing a book that is as long as the Christian New Testament. He finished elementary school at the age of twelve but had to delay starting middle school for two years because of the revolution of 1919.

When he was fourteen, Qutb went to live with his uncle in Cairo, where he completed middle school and high school. He was in his last year of middle school when the caliphate fell in 1924. In 1929, Qutb enrolled in the teacher's college, Darul Oloom, and started his career in 1933 as an Arabic language teacher for the Egyptian ministry of education, which he continued until 1939. He became well known as a literary critic.[4] Qutb described that period of his life as a time of disbelief when he questioned and doubted Allah—why did Allah allow the Muslim government (the caliphate) to collapse in that horrible way?

Let's compare what Qutb and Mawdudi were doing in their twenties. Mawdudi was already engaged in Islamist activity while Qutb was working with education and literature. However, they did have one important similarity: they were both engaged in writing. Soon their paths would cross.

Gifted writers

In 1932 Mawdudi established a Muslim magazine called *Turjurman al-Qur'an* [The Translator of the Quran]. It reached every part of the Muslim world. Starting in 1937, Mawdudi published a new book almost every year, discussing his vision of the revival of Islam. His most influential books include the six-volume *Tafhimul Qur'an* [Understanding the Quran], published in 1972, which has impacted Muslims all over the world. Other books include *Towards Understanding Islam, Let Us Be Muslims, Way to the Qur'an, The Islamic Movement,* and *The Islamic Way of Life.*

Sayyid Qutb was surely reading these books. In 1941, Mawdudi established a new radical Muslim movement, Jema'at e-Islami, declaring that the war to bring back the glory of Islam would begin in India and spread over the entire world. In 1947 this group succeeded in declaring independence for the Indian states with a Muslim majority, and the country of Pakistan was born.

Meanwhile, starting in 1939, Qutb became a functionary in Egypt's Ministry of Education and started to write for newspapers and magazines on a new topic: the philosophy of Islam. In 1945 he published his first two books about the Quran. In 1948 the government sent him to the United States to study the educational system, which proved to be a major turning point in Qutb's life.

Qutb described his experience in the United States in very negative terms. He said of the American citizen:

> His behavior reminds us of the era of the caveman. He is primitive in the way he lusts after power, ignoring ideals and manners and principles.[5]

After visiting a church dance, he complained, "The dance floor was replete with tapping feet, enticing legs, arms wrapped around waists, lips pressed to lips, and chests pressed to chests. The atmosphere was full of desire..."[6]

Qutb returned to Egypt in 1950 when he was forty-six years old and re-created himself as a radical Muslim to push back against the evil influences of the West. He began a solid relationship with many leaders and young members of the Muslim Brotherhood, including Gemal Abdul Nasser.

At this point, both Qutb and Mawdudi were convinced that the only solution for the problems of the Islamic world was to establish an Islamic government and to institute Islamic law. As they put this belief in action, both men would find themselves betrayed by their leaders.

Double-crossed!

Mawdudi and his movement successfully created a new country called Pakistan, but secular politics stole his dream of Islamic revolution. Gulam Muhammad became the leader of Pakistan, and then he refused to apply Islamic law. So Mawdudi and his movement turned against him. In 1948, Mawdudi gave a strong speech in the law school in Lahore (Ghulam's childhood hometown) and called on Muslims in Pakistan to establish the political system according to Islamic law. A few months later Gulam Muhammad arrested Mawdudi and the other leaders of his movement. Mawdudi spent twenty months in jail and was released in 1950.

A few years later, Qutb experienced a similar event. Qutb and the Muslim Brotherhood joined with Nasser and his military group to overthrow the Egyptian government led by King Farouk. But when Nasser was in power, he turned against the Muslim Brotherhood when they demanded that he instate Islamic law. Because of his relationship with Nasser, for a time Qutb attempted to persuade him, and he accepted a position as minister of education. Nasser ordered that the books and writings of Sayyid Qutb be taught in the public schools. Ultimately, the relationship between Nasser and Qutb deteriorated when Qutb realized there was no hope for Nasser to implement Islamic law, and in 1954 Qutb quit his position and took part in an unsuccessful plot by the Muslim Brotherhood to assassinate Nasser. Qutb, along with many others, was sentenced to prison with hard labor and remained in Tarah prison south of Cairo for about ten years.[7]

Violence against inmates was common. In June 1957, Nasser ordered prison wardens to shoot hundreds of Muslim Brotherhood prisoners in their cells. Seeing prisoners killed in front of his eyes radicalized Qutb and his writings.

Now let's see how Mawdudi's and Qutb's lives came to an end.

Their legacies

After Mawdudi was released, he continued to lead the rebellion against the Pakistani government, causing great riots, so the police arrested him again in 1953. They gave him the death sentence, but his movement caused such trouble in the country that the government changed the sentence from death to life in prison. His group never stopped protesting until he was released in 1955. Mawdudi traveled and spoke frequently in England, which laid the foundation for the strong radical movement that exists there today. In 1979, at the age of seventy-six, he died, leaving behind more than seventy books about Islamic issues and a huge spiritual influence over the Islamic world.

The Egyptian government kept Qutb in prison for his full sentence until 1964. While in prison, Qutb was consumed with writing. He put together a massive, thirty-volume commentary on the Quran that remains influential to this day. He also wrote the text of his most famous book, *Milestones Along the Road*, and smuggled it out of prison bit by bit through friends. It was finally published in 1964. In it, Qutb called for the "revival of Islam" with the eloquence developed through years of writing and literary critique.[8] Rather than focus on specific complaints against the Egyptian government, Qutb laid out a broad philosophy of the methods whereby Islamic law can be instituted worldwide. Because of his writing talent, the book can easily cross generational and national boundaries, which makes it the more dangerous. Its influence can easily be seen in the writers that followed him.

Because of this book, the Egyptian government executed Qutb in 1965, but his philosophy and influence never died. They spread throughout the Islamic world.

The Relationship Between Qutb and Mawdudi

The main point about Mawdudi and Qutb is that it took both of them to produce the huge influence that is still felt today. Qutb drew from Mawdudi's philosophy to develop key concepts that he immortalized through the power of his writing. Two of the most important concepts were:

1. Modern society defined as *jahilliyyah*
2. The need for a vanguard to re-Islamize society

First, there is the new definition of *jahiliyyah*. *Jahiliyyah* is an Islamic concept referring to the spiritual condition of pre-Islamic Arabian society. It is described as a state of ignorance of God's message.[9] In Muhammad's time this word had been used in reference to the people living before Islam was revealed. Medieval scholar Ibn Taymiyyah revised the definition to include the king of the Mongols, who had converted to Islam but still used the Yasa code of law rather than Islamic law (*sharia*). Mawdudi took it a step further and defined the new *jahiliyya* as the bulk of the world's Muslims because they were accepting laws and government that were not based exclusively on Islam. In other words, if a Muslim or Muslim government did not implement Islamic law alone, they were apostate, and the true believer must wage jihad against them.[10]

Second, a vanguard must be prepared to re-Islamize society. This group would follow the example Muhammad set between the time he received his revelation and the time the Muslim state was established in Medina. Qutb believed the vanguard would begin with a period of weakness, separate themselves from the *jahili* society, gather strength, and then return with sufficient power to establish the Muslim state.

Conclusion

Through al-Banna, Mawdudi, and Qutb, the Great Awakening of Islamic fundamentalism was established. Next, a younger generation would take these ideas, radicalize them further, and start a new era of violence in the Islamic world. I call these men the Evangelists.

THE EVANGELISTS

	Dr. Salah Sariah	Shokri Mustafa	Abdul Salam Faraj
Birth/death	1933–1975	1942–1978	1954–1982
Nationality	Palestinian	Egyptian	Egyptian
Education	Doctorate in scientific education	Studied agricultural sciences	Electrical engineer
Name of group	Started Egyptian branch of Hizb al-Tahrir (Islamic Liberation Movement), 1974	Founded al-Takfir wal-Hijra (Emigration and Flight), 1971	Helped to start Egyptian Al-Jihad (branch of Al-Gama'a al-Islamiyyah), 1979
Key Publications	*The Message of Faith*, 1973	*Al Kalafa* [The Leader]; transcript of legal defense, 1978	*The Abandoned Duty*, 1981
Unique Message	Detailed argument that Muslims in general have fallen into apostasy	Separation from infidel Muslim society; intolerant of anyone not involved in al-Takfir wal-Hijra	Detailed argument that jihad is the only effective way to establish Islamic government and law
Crime	Invaded military training school in Cairo, 1974	Kidnapped and killed moderate Muslim preacher, 1977	Helped to plan assassination of Egyptian President Sadat, 1981
Type of death	Executed by Egyptian government	Hanged by Egyptian government	Executed by Egyptian government
Age at death	41	36	28
Status of group today	Banned in Egypt, legal in England. Arabic Web site in 2005 called for "physical battle against the infidel rulers in the Islamic world." British branch claims to reject violence.	Active in most Arab nations. Al-Qaeda leader Ayman al-Zawahiri and Iraqi terrorist leader al-Zarqawi are thought to be linked to these sects. Considered extreme.	Egyptian Al-Jihad merged with Al-Qaeda under the leadership of Ayman al-Zawahiri.

4
THE EVANGELISTS

After the execution of Qutb, a new generation of leaders rose up to take the message of jihad to the people. Unlike Qutb and Mawdudi, these leaders did not have formal religious training. However, they studied the Quran, the sunnah, and Islamic law for themselves and vowed to take action on it. They were also greatly influenced by the writings of the Founders.

Just as Christianity has evangelists, these men were evangelists to the Muslim world, calling people to the true faith as they perceived it. Just as Christians form "para-church" ministries to focus on a particular mission, these men formed "para-mosque" radical groups to help them fight jihad. The three key evangelists of the new radical movement were Dr. Salah Sariah, Shokri Moustafa, and Abdul Salam Faraj.

These men were executed within a few years of each other, but their groups did not die. As you will learn, they are alive today through Hizb al-Tahrir, al-Takfir wal-Hijra, Al-Jihad, and Al-Qaeda.

Dr. Salah Sariah: Proving Apostasy

Born near Haifa in 1933, Dr. Salah Sariah was a Palestinian with a doctorate in scientific education. Sariah lived in Jordan until 1970 and eventually made his way to Cairo.[1] In 1973 he published a powerful booklet titled *The Message of Faith,* in which he condemned the general Muslim population as apostate.

Dr. Sariah introduced his book dramatically:

> This study is the first one—as far as I can tell—of its kind in trying to diagnose the apostasy that Muslims have fallen into, either knowingly or unknowingly, due to the new circumstances that

> surrounded them, and its importance exceeds, in my opinion, by a thousand times the importance of studying the old cases.[2]

In other words, Dr. Sariah accepted the call from al-Banna, Mawdudi, and Qutb to violently confront apostate government and society. However, Dr. Sariah wanted to present more specific information to prove that the way Muslims believed and behaved was truly apostate. His book focused on that goal.

Dr. Sariah wanted to make sure his discussion resulted in action, not just talk. He complained:

> Muslims with the Quran resemble an army leader who lays out a full plan to fight his enemy, but instead of executing the plan, the army reads the plan, accepts it, kisses it, and hangs it on the wall until the next day.[3]

Even though I am no longer a Muslim, when I read the book today I can easily see how susceptible Muslims are persuaded by the intensity of his language and his message.

In 1974 Dr. Sariah also imported a new radical group to Egypt. He and a fellow Palestinian founded the Egyptian branch of Hizb al-Tahrir (Islamic Liberation Movement). He acted as the leader for training in military arts. Like the radicals who came before him, Dr. Sariah's goal was to find the most effective way to overturn and destroy any governments that did not completely comply with Islamic law, including existing Muslim countries.

On April 19, 1974, Dr. Sariah and his movement invaded a military training institute in Cairo, hoping to establish a base from which to overturn the government. The Egyptian authorities responded with great force and arrested him and all of the members of his movement. In October 1975 the federal government of Egypt sentenced Dr. Sariah and many of his followers to death.

It has been thirty years since that event, and Hizb al-Tahrir is still active in several countries. Each group has their specific philosophy. For example, the British group rejects violence but at the same time condemns freedom, democracy, and any form of participation in the British political system.[4]

On the other hand, a homepage for a Hizb al-Tahrir branch in Arabic stated the following goals:

> [We are] committed to enter a physical battle against the infidel rulers in the Islamic world and to expose their infidelity against Islam and hold them accountable to Islamic law.
>
> The main goal for Hizb al-Tahrir is to establish the Islamic state and bring the calipha system back to life in the Islamic world after destroying all the images of the infidel political systems.[5]

Dr. Sariah is dead, but his ideas live on.

Shokri Mustafa: Separation From Infidels

Shokri Moustafa was an intense personality who started out studying agriculture and ended up leading his radical group into the desert to grow their own crops and set up a self-sufficient community.

Shokri was born in 1942 in Egypt, and he was first arrested for distributing Muslim Brotherhood literature at his agricultural college in 1965 when he was twenty-three years old. Under Nasser's strict policies, he was imprisoned for the next six years. Just like Qutb, he was probably kept in bad conditions and tortured, which hardened him and further radicalized him. In prison he became involved in a Muslim Brotherhood splinter group called the Muslim Society (Jama'at al-Muslimun) that practiced a particularly strict interpretation of Qutb's *Milestones Along the Road*. The group even separated itself from other prisoners that it deemed to be infidel for collaborating with the government.[6]

In the early 1970s, in order to resist Communism in Egypt, Anwar Sadat, the next Egyptian president, made a decision to release many imprisoned members of radical groups. President Sadat even had Sayyid Qutb's book *Milestones Along the Road* republished at this time because it criticized Communism! The radicals successfully resisted Communism, but Sadat did not realize that they soon would challenge his authority as well.

Shokri was released in 1971 and finished his university studies while forming a new chapter of Jama'at al-Muslimun outside of prison. He recruited members among college students and graduates.

Shokri met with Dr. Sariah once in the early 1970s to discuss merging their respective groups, but although they had similar goals, their ideologies were too different.[7]

Even among radical groups, Shokri's group stood out as extreme. Anyone who was not a member of their group was infidel. They believed in separating themselves completely from what they considered the corrupt Egyptian society and refused to pray with people who were not in their group. Members lived as a group in caves in Upper Egypt where they established a self-sufficient community and farm in the desert, or they lived as a group in apartments in Cairo.

Journalists began to refer to the group as *al-Takfir wal-Hijra*. *Takfir* means "to declare someone an infidel," and *hijra* is the word that refers to Muhammad's migration from the hostile Mecca to the welcoming Medina. Taken together, they can be translated as "Condemnation [of Muslim Society] and Flight."

The members were planning to increase their numbers and reach the point of power that would enable them to overturn the government and establish an Islamic nation. Other radicals criticized them, however, for refusing to fight until their preparation was complete.[8]

Theologically, Shokri insisted on interpreting the Quran and hadith directly rather than looking to Muslim scholars for guidance.[9] This was a dramatic departure from societal norm.

In 1977 Shokri and his group attacked Cairo nightclubs, and in 1978 they kidnapped a moderate professor from Al-Azhar University and murdered him. In response, the government arrested Shokri and four hundred members of his movement. Shokri was convicted and executed that same year at the age of thirty-six.[10]

Al-Takfir wal-Hijra did not die with Shokri. Under Ayman al-Zawahiri's leadership, Al-Qaeda followed Shokri's example of separation and preparation by setting up training camps with the permission of the Taliban in Afghanistan. As reported by *The Observer*, a daily British Internet newspaper in 2001, Osama bin Laden was also financing Takfir groups in Europe who were planning more spectacular attacks that would follow the 9/11 event.[11]

ABDUL SALAM FARAJ: PASSION OF YOUTH

Muhammad Abdul Salam Faraj was well aware of Shokri Moustafa's execution in 1978 and the decimation of his group. At that time, Faraj was twenty-four years old and already active in the Muslim Brotherhood. He followed in the footsteps of his father, who was also a Muslim Brotherhood member. Faraj, like the other two evangelists of jihad, did not have a religious education. He worked as an electrical engineer at Cairo University.[12]

This lack of religious training pushed all of the evangelists of jihad further into fundamentalism. They simply took the words of the Quran and the hadith and applied them to modern times. They also quoted Islamic scholars who supported their fundamentalist point of view.

Faraj became frustrated and impatient with the Muslim Brotherhood, and he drifted away to participate in other radical groups. He finally discovered Al-Gama'a al-Islamiyyah, which was founded at Cairo University in 1978 by Essam al-Aryan, a student in the school of medicine, and Helmy al-Jazar.

In 1980, the Muslim Brotherhood invited Al-Gama'a to merge together with them in order to increase their effectiveness. At the same time, the Muslim Brotherhood did not want to act immediately to overthrow the Egyptian government by force. Al-Gama'a was split between those who wanted to join the Muslim Brotherhood and those who wanted to take immediate action against the government. (I described this bloody conflict in my first book, *Islam and Terrorism.*) Faraj went with the group who wanted action.

During that time, the top leader of the Muslim Brotherhood, Mustafa Mash'hor, published a book titled *Preachers, Not Judges,* in which he called for Muslims to use politics, preaching, and education to change the government rather than force. As a university student, I remember members of radical groups making fun of this book for laying down power for preaching. "Preaching won't work without power," they said. "You can't enforce Islamic law without power."

In reaction to the "persuasion philosophy," in 1981 Faraj wrote a short and powerful book titled *Al-Farida al Ghai'iba* [The Abandoned Duty]. This book was the founding document of a new branch of Al-Gama'a al-Islamiyyah focused on radical operations. Calling themselves Al-Jihad, they would seize the attention of the world before the year ended.

Faraj was only twenty-eight years old when he wrote his manifesto declaring that the Islamic world had neglected the sixth pillar of Islam: the duty of jihad. His passions ran high, and in no case did compromise, failure, or moderation taint his logic. He was utterly convinced of the truth of his cause.

Faraj acknowledged that some of his peers opposed trying to overthrow the government immediately because his group lacked strength and the government could react and "destroy everything we have accomplished so far." His response was:

> Establishing the nation of Islam is an execution of the orders of Allah, and we are not required to show results.... As soon as the government of the infidels collapses, everything will be in the hands of the Muslims, making it impossible for anyone to take it back.... The laws of Islam are just and they will find a sure welcome even from those who do not know Islam.... Allah says: "O you who believe! If you will help (the cause of) Allah, He will help you and make your feet firm. [Surah 47:7]."[13]

He believed that if his group acted, Allah would supernaturally help them. Faraj wrote:

> ...In all previous nations, Allah used to bring his punishment upon the infidels, and the enemies of his religion through natural causes, such as earthquakes, or drowning, or screaming, or by wind. This situation is different to the nation of Mohammad, for He the Glorified has addressed them, saying: "Fight them; Allah will punish them by your hands and bring them to disgrace, and assist you against them and heal the hearts of a believing people" [Surah 9:14], which means that a Muslim must first take the matter of Jihad upon himself, then Allah will interfere through the natural causes, to accomplish victory at the hands of the believers which comes from Allah.[14]

Faraj recruited for Al-Jihad mainly in the poor quarters of Cairo where he preached Friday sermons. However, he also recruited essential members from the presidential guard, military intelligence, civil bureaucracy, and university students.

One of his most important recruits was a young man in his late twenties named Ayman al-Zawahiri, who is now well known as the second in command of Al-Qaeda. The group grew rapidly, taking in other radical groups (including former al-Takfir wal-Hijra cells), and began carrying out terrorist attacks against the state. They terrorized and robbed Christian businesses to raise money.[15]

In the fall of 1981, Faraj and his group had an idea to assassinate Sadat and the top leaders of Egypt, thereby paving the way to establish an Islamic government with Islamic law. The planning hastily took place at a mosque in Cairo. They decided that the longer they waited or planned, the more likely they would be to encounter failure or betrayal. So Faraj assembled a team within ten days, and, on October 6, 1981, an undercover military sharpshooter shot and killed President Anwar Sadat during a military parade.

However, Faraj's lack of planning was their downfall. No supernatural aid came from Allah to help them. Vice President Hosni Mubarek quickly took charge and easily rounded up the Al-Jihad members. On April 15, 1982, Faraj, the sharpshooter, and three others were put to death. Faraj was twenty-eight years old.

Thousands more Al-Gama'a members were imprisoned, including Abod Zoummar and two of his friends, Karam Zohdy and Assim Abdul Maghed, who were all senior leaders in Al-Jihad. You will want to remember these three names because they are very important in the next wave of radical writings.

Faraj's life was short, but the group he founded survived and would later play a role in the attack that caught the attention of the whole world. You see, Ayman al-Zawahiri was one of the Al-Jihad members who was arrested after Sadat's assassination, but the government was only able to keep him in prison for three years on weapons charges. When he was released in 1984 he eventually became allied with Osama bin Laden. Starting in early 1998, Egyptian Al-Jihad received most of its funding from Al-Qaeda, and by June 2001, Al-Jihad and Al-Qaeda became one.[16]

Conclusion

Impulsiveness and passion marked this phase of the development of Islamic radicalism. These three writers followed the same path. First, they developed a unique philosophy and gathered a small, committed group around them. Then they made an attempt to overthrow the Egyptian government by force and were met with overwhelming resistance. In the end, the government executed the top leaders and locked up the group members in prison. An incredible number of radicals were incarcerated. The exact number is not publicly known, but estimates range from ten thousand to twenty thousand.[17]

When Al-Gama'a members went to military court, they thought of themselves as heroes who would change the destiny of the Islamic world. They quoted a famous hadith of Muhammad, saying they were the fulfillment of his prophecy:

> The youth bring me victory and the elders have failed me.

Al-Gama'a members saw the Muslim Brotherhood era ending, and they expected the Brotherhood to fail. Even in prison, the Al-Gama'a leaders remained defiant and carried on their leadership of the rebellion from behind bars for the next fifteen years. From inside Egyptian prisons the next generation of writers would emerge.

THE PRISONERS

	Abod Zoummar	Karam Zohdy	Assim Abdul Maghed
Birth	1946	1952	Unknown
Nationality	Egyptian	Egyptian	Egyptian
Education	Military	Agricultural engineer	Civil engineer
Group Affiliation	Al-Jihad, Al-Gama'a al-Islamiyyah	Al-Jihad, Al-Gama'a al-Islamiyyah	Al-Jihad, Al-Gama'a al-Islamiyyah
Key Publication	Author of *The Strategy of Al-Jihad*; coauthor of the *Constitution of Al-Jihad*, 1986	Coauthor of the *Constitution of Al-Jihad*, 1986	Coauthor of the *Constitution of Al-Jihad*, 1986
Original Message	Overturn immoral ruler; fig ththose who oppose *sharia*; establish caliphate	Overturn immoral ruler; fight those who oppose *sharia*; establish caliphate	Overturn immoral ruler; fight those who oppose *sharia*; establish caliphate
Crimes	Planning assassination of Sadat; acts of terrorism	Planning assassination of Sadat; acts of terrorism	Planning assassination of Sadat; acts of terrorism
Length of incarceration	1981– (Not released as of July 2005. Fifteen-year sentence is completed.)	1981–September 2003 (22 years) He was 51 years old when he was released.	1981–September 2003 (22 years)
Current philosophy	Ran for president of Egypt on a 50-point program; still committed to original goals	Leading Al-Gama'a to reject violence in favor of nonviolent persuasion; still committed to original goals	Leading Al-Gama'a to reject violence in favor of nonviolent persuasion; still committed to original goals

5

THE PRISONERS

When Islamic fundamentalism was sweeping Egypt, three friends from southern Egypt answered the call together. They joined Al-Jihad and rose in leadership, but there was no escape from President Mubarek's crackdown after their coup in 1981 failed. Thousands of radicals were incarcerated in the notorious Egyptian prison system—including the three friends from southern Egypt.

The three young men were Abod Zoummar, Karam Zohdy, and Assim Abdel Maghed.

It has long been known that torture is a routine practice in prisons, police stations, and State Security Investigations (SSI) offices in Egypt. Even the government-appointed National Council for Human Rights (NCHR) acknowledges that torture is part of "normal investigative practice in Egypt."[1]

It was the first time in prison for these men in their late twenties and mid-thirties—and their first taste of torture. That kind of situation either breaks a person or hardens him. In their case, they were hardened.

Before the assassination of President Sadat, they were busy with jihad, and didn't have the time to write. Now all they had was time. Out of anger and bitterness they drafted the *Constitution of Al-Jihad* to declare to the world that what they did was right and that they would try again to overthrow the infidel government. Handwritten, page by page, the manuscripts were smuggled out of the prison and published in 1986.

Zoummar, the former military leader, also produced his own book titled *Strategy of Al-Jihad* with practical information about training people to overthrow the government and how to run the country afterward.

Their sympathizers took the handwritten pages and made copies, passing them from hand to hand all over Egypt.

Hear the defiant voice of Zoummar from inside prison:

> So would you repent, O rulers of the homelands in Egypt, you who have prevented the law of Allah from being applied in His land and upon His people...
>
> Is it not the time for you to step aside after your failure, and make way for the men of the Islamic movements to lead the nation to its goodness and maturity by establishing the nation of Islam according to the prophetic fashion...[2]

Zoummar and the others vowed to carry on the fight no matter what the cost.

> Our way is the way of sacrifice, giving, and redemption...material things become cheap. In it life, money, and everything of value will be sacrificed so that we can relay the word of truth, and raise high the banner of Islam to shine anew the sun of Islam.
>
> Thousands upon thousands of people who came before us have marched on this road; honorable men of integrity whose martyrdom has been like glowing lights and guiding posts to whoever sought Allah and the final day.[3]

During the 1980s, the members of Al-Jihad and Al-Gama'a al-Islamiyyah who were not incarcerated continued their attacks against the government. In 1992, Al-Gama'a began a new, more aggressive campaign than they had conducted in the 1980s. They launched shooting attacks against tourists' buses and assassinated Dr. Farag Foda, a prominent Egyptian politician and former speaker of the Egyptian Parliament. The attacks against tourists' buses were a serious economic blow to Egypt's economy, with tourist earnings dropping by an estimated 50 percent by 1993. In 1994 Al-Gama'a bombed a series of banks, and in 1995 they attempted to assassinate President Hosni Mubarek while he was in Ethiopia. They robbed Christian jewelry stores to finance their operations.[4]

While the prison leaders were trying to mastermind the defeat of the Egyptian government, the radical Egyptian leaders outside the country were developing a new philosophy that would completely change the fight. It was the philosophy that produced 9/11 and brought the entire world into conflict with Islamic radicalism. And it was birthed through the collaboration of two men of privilege: Ayman al-Zawahiri from Egypt and Osama bin Laden from Saudi Arabia. They are the Aristocrats of radical Islam and the masterminds behind global terrorism.

THE ARISTOCRATS[1]

	Osama bin Laden	Ayman al-Zawahiri
Birth Date	July 30, 1957, the 17th of 52 brothers and sisters borne by multiple wives	June 1, 1951
Birth Place	Saudi Arabia	Egypt
Family Background	His father came from Yemen to Saudi Arabia around 1930 as a laborer. From that beginning, the bin Laden family built the largest construction company in the kingdom and was awarded contracts to renovate the three holiest mosques in the Islamic world.	Zawahiri's family was distinguished both on his father's and mother's side. His grandfather was the imam of Al-Azhar Mosque in Cairo, and his father was a professor of pharmacology. His maternal grandfather was president of Cairo University and ambassador for the Egyptian government.
Education	Public administration degree from King Abdul-Aziz University in Jeddah, Saudi Arabia, 1981	MD degree from Cairo University, cum laude, 1974, master's degree in surgery, 1978
Name of Group	Founded Al-Qaeda in 1988 to channel fighters and funds to jihad in Afghanistan	Second in command of Al-Qaeda; leader of Egyptian Al-Jihad, which began to merge with Al-Qaeda in 1998
Imprisonment	None	Arrested and imprisoned in 1981 after assassination of Sadat. Released in 1984. He was hardened and radicalized by torture and poor conditions in prison.
Key Publications	*Fatwa Against Jews and Crusaders*, 1998 *Letter to America, 2000* (These documents were authorized by bin Laden but not necessarily written by him entirely.)	*Knights Under the Banner of the Prophet* (his memoirs, 2001) *Healing the Chest of the Believer* (1986) *The Prohibiting Word*
Unique Message	Attack the far enemy instead of the near enemy	Use of suicide bombers as a primary method of attack
Jihad Activity	Started at the age of 22 in Afghanistan; total of 26 years to date.	Started at the age of 16 in Egypt; total of 38 years to date.
Personal Life	Three or four wives; at least fifteen children	One wife; four daughters and a son

6
THE ARISTOCRATS

Osama bin Laden and Ayman al-Zawahiri are different from any of the radicals who preceded them in the modern revival of Islamicism. They are not scholars, like the founders, even though al-Zawahiri writes scholarly papers. They are not evangelists, like the young men who launched doomed attacks against Egypt and were executed without making much impact. They are not prisoners, like the authors of the *Constitution of Al-Jihad,* who lived defiantly but in bondage in Egyptian prison.

These two men had the potential to live comfortably and build up their communities and nations. Yet they left behind ease, wealth, and respectability to become experts at suicide bombing and random killing of non-Muslims and Muslims. They are the aristocrats of radical Islam.

Infamous Duo

People in America see Osama bin Laden as the leader of the infamous terrorist group Al-Qaeda and therefore as the most important figure in Islamic radicalism today. However, the fact is that bin Laden would not hold his position of power today without the partnership with Ayman al-Zawahiri. This chapter will describe:

- The privileged pedigrees of these two men
- How bin Laden and al-Zawahiri came together in Afghanistan
- How the United States provided funding for them to fight the Russians in Afghanistan during the 1980s

- The powerful, irreversible changes that Al-Qaeda has brought to the radical movement, including al-Zawahiri's teaching notes about suicide bombing

Bin Laden (b. 1957) turns forty-eight years old in 2005, and al-Zawahiri (b. 1951) turns fifty-four. Between them, they have been active jihadists for sixty-four years. Jihad has been their career for virtually their entire adult lives. It is all they know or want to know. They are hardened, seasoned, paranoid, and extreme.

Privileged Backgrounds

If you were going to make a broad comparison, you could say the bin Laden family of Saudi Arabia had no lack of wealth and the al-Zawahiri family in Egypt had no lack of prestige.

Bin Laden's father, Muhammad bin Oud bin Laden, emigrated from Yemen to Saudi Arabia around 1930 as a poor, low-class laborer. In the 1950s he became close to the royal family and demonstrated his skill at engineering and construction. In 1964 he was awarded the contract to build practically all of the roads in the country.

Muhammad died in a helicopter crash in 1967 when Osama was only ten years old. However, the eldest son carried on the family business. Their crowning achievement was the contract to rebuild the Islamic holy sites at Mecca and Medina with funds from the kingdom's new oil wealth. When that son died, the next eldest son took over leadership. Currently the company employs some thirty-two thousand people in thirty countries. Osama bin Laden inherited a share of this family fortune.

In contrast, there was no monetary fortune for al-Zawahiri to inherit, but he did have a fortune in prestige both from his father's and his mother's families.

> His grandfather, Sheikh Al-Ahmadi Al-Zawahiri was the [Great] Imam of Al-Azhar in Cairo. His father, Muhammad Rabi' Al-Zawahiri was a professor of pharmacology at Ein Shams University who passed away in 1995. His maternal grandfather, Abd Al-Wahab Azzam, was a professor of oriental literature and president of Cairo University as well as the Egyptian ambassador to Pakistan, Saudi Arabia, and Yemen, and was so known for his piety that he was referred to as "the devout ambassador." His

grandfather's brother, Abd Al-Rahman Azzam [pasha], became the first Secretary General of the Arab League.[2]

Bin Laden: Finding Jihad in Afghanistan

Osama married his first wife at the age of seventeen. He went on to attend King Abdul Azziz University in Jidda where he took mandatory courses in Islamic studies from a powerful preacher of Islamic revivalism named Abdullah Azzam, who has a doctorate in Islamic law from Al-Azhar University. When the Soviet Union invaded Afghanistan in 1979, Azzam produced a *fatwa* declaring both the Afghan and Palestinian struggles to be *jihads.*[3] Azzam founded an organization to help the jihad fighters, and Osama caught the vision. He visited Afghanistan shortly after the invasion to see refugees and meet leaders; he returned to Saudi Arabia to raise money to support the jihad fighters. He collected a huge amount of money and donations and returned to Afghanistan to deliver it.[4]

In 1982 bin Laden started spending more and more time in Afghanistan, and in 1984 he established a guesthouse for those coming from other countries to join in the jihad. In 1986 bin Laden began building training camps in Afghanistan and personally commanding battle. He was in charge of six major battles and hundreds of small operations. In other words, he wasn't just writing checks; his "boots were on the ground."

In 1988 bin Laden founded an organization he called Al-Qaeda, or "the Base," to help keep track of the fighters coming into the country so he could report on their whereabouts to their families.

In 1989, after ten years of fighting, the Soviets pulled out of Afghanistan. It was a costly victory for jihad. More than a million Afghans—8 percent of the country's population—had been killed.[5]

Al-Zawahiri: Al-Qaeda's Key Recruiter

While bin Laden began his jihad activity at the fairly young age of twenty-two, al-Zawahiri seemed to be going in that direction from his youth. In his biography on the Zarqawi Web site, al-Zawahiri described how he started his involvement with radical groups at the age of fifteen.

> My beginning of Islamic activity was with [Al-Gama'a al-Islamiyyah, which later produced] Al-Jihad, which I am proud

> to be a member of. And this was in 1966 A.D. when that group was established after the death of the martyr Sayyid Qutb, mercy of Allah be upon him.[6]

Al-Zawahiri later praised Qutb as "the first spark of the Islamic radical movement" and described Qutb's book *Milestones Along the Road* as "the real and original constitution of Muslim radical groups."[7]

Though he was involved in radical activity, al-Zawahiri continued his education and his life. He graduated from medical school at Cairo University in 1974, took over leadership of his radical cell in 1975, and married his first and only wife in 1978.

Al-Zawahiri visited Afghanistan for the first time in 1980 when he was invited to go with another doctor to provide medical help to injured fighters. When al-Zawahiri came back, he had a revealing conversation with an old friend, who recalled:

> "He started off by saying that the Americans were the real enemy and had to be confronted," Schleifer told me. "I said, 'I don't understand. You just came back from Afghanistan, where you're cooperating with the Americans. Now you're saying America is the enemy?'"
>
> "Sure, we're taking American help to fight the Russians," Zawahiri replied. "But they're equally evil."

In the beginning of the 1980s, Abod Zoummar introduced al-Zawahiri to the Egyptian Al-Jihad group, which he joined and quickly rose in authority. Al-Zawahiri's ultimate goal was to overthrow the Egyptian government and establish an Islamic state. He wrote in his memoir that he and his group began collecting weapons and storing them at his medical clinic. However, government officials caught a man carrying a load of guns and, consequently, arrested more than fifteen hundred people, including most of the Al-Jihad leaders, though al-Zawahiri was not captured.

However, without al-Zawahiri's knowledge, Faraj's cell had hastily conceived a plan to assassinate President Anwar Sadat, which they did on October 6, 1981. Al-Zawahiri wrote that he was not even aware of the plan until a few hours before it was executed, and he was dismayed because of the lack of planning. Al-Zawahiri was arrested a few weeks later. He wasn't convicted in the assassination of Sadat, but he was convicted on weapons charges and sentenced to three years in prison.

Al-Zawahiri may be doing something different today if he had not spent those three years in prison. Sources say al-Zawahiri was embarrassed and humiliated by the prison torture, during which he gave information that led to the arrest and imprisonment of one of his trusted operatives, Qamari. The man was later killed in a shoot-out with the police after escaping from prison.[8]

Al-Zawahiri was deeply angered at the treatment of the jihadist prisoners. During the group trial in 1982, he stood out from the three hundred other defendants in the long cage that held them in the courtroom. Al-Zawahiri addressed the court for them all.

> The prisoners pull off their shoes and raise their robes to expose the marks of torture. Zawahiri talks about the torture that took place in the "dirty Egyptian jails…where we suffered the severest inhuman treatment. There they kicked us, they beat us, they whipped us with electric cables, they shocked us with electricity! They shocked us with electricity! And they used the wild dogs! And they used the wild dogs! And they hung us over the edges of the doors"—here he bends over to demonstrate—"with our hands tied at the back! They arrested the wives, the mothers, the fathers, the sisters, and the sons!"
>
> Zawahiri calls out the names of several prisoners who, he says, died as a result of torture. "So where is democracy?" he shouts. "Where is freedom? Where is human rights? Where is justice? Where is justice? We will never forget! We will never forget!"[9]

Al-Zawahiri was released from prison after completing his sentence in 1984. He wrote:

> After my release from prison, I started bringing the brothers together once again, and we decided to take advantage of the great opportunities in Afghanistan to train many members of the Muslim youth, and Allah helped us in this in a great way.[10]

By 1987, one of al-Zawahiri's brothers and another colleague joined him from Egypt, and the three of them reorganized Egyptian Al-Jihad. Al-Zawahiri recruited more jihad fighters from Egypt and worked to make a strong relationship between bin Laden and himself.[11]

Warriors Without a War

After the Soviets pulled out of Afghanistan in 1989, both al-Zawahiri and bin Laden spent several years trying to find a new method for carrying out their goals. Bin Laden ended up in Sudan in 1992, and al-Zawahiri followed.[12] However, they were not completely in agreement about their goals. Al-Zawahiri focused on reviving Al-Jihad and trying to overthrow the Egyptian government. Bin Laden "sought to merge all Islamic terrorist groups into a single multinational corporation," and he focused attacks on U.S. military forces.[13]

Ultimately, after the Taliban took over in Afghanistan, both bin Laden and al-Zawahiri returned. They continued operations, and in 1998 they crystallized their strategy in their most famous fatwa.

1998 Fatwa Against Jews and Crusaders

In 1998 bin Laden issued a fiery call to jihad titled "Fatwa Against Jews and Crusaders." (A *fatwa* is a legal opinion from an Islamic religious leader.) It was signed by al-Zawahiri, representing Al-Jihad of Egypt, as well as three other high leaders of major jihad groups. This document is 1,100 words long, and it shows how Al-Qaeda justify what they do. They claimed that the United States (known as "the Crusaders") had declared war against Islam; therefore, any Muslim was justified in fighting back. Al-Qaeda said the United States declared war in three ways:

1. By establishing and maintaining military bases in Saudi Arabia during the first Gulf War (1990–1991). This is an affront to Islam by allowing non-Muslims in the Holy Land where Muhammad established Islam. (Mecca and Medina are located in Saudi Arabia.)

2. By waging war against Iraq and Saddam Hussein after Iraq invaded Kuwait. The fatwa claimed that one million Iraqi were killed, which is a grossly inflated number. According to "Gulf War Air Power Survey" by Thomas A. Keaney and Eliot A. Cohen (a report commissioned by the U.S. Air Force; 1993; ISBN 0-16-041950-6), there were an estimated 10,000–12,000 Iraqi combat deaths in the air campaign and as many as 10,000 casualties in

the ground war. This analysis is based on enemy prisoner of war reports. The Iraqi government claimed that 2,300 civilians died during the air campaign.[14]

3. By supporting the survival of the state of Israel through "destroying" Iraq and "weakening" other states in the region.

Therefore the fatwa declared: "The ruling to kill the Americans and their allies—civilians and military—is an individual duty for every Muslim who can do it in any country in which it is possible to do it." Beyond killing Americans, the fatwa also called for Muslims to "plunder their money wherever and whenever they find it." The idea of plundering the conquered comes directly from Muhammad's example of conquering the neighboring tribes around him, taking the belongings, and selling the women and children as slaves. (You may read my book *Jesus and Muhammad* for a good overview of Muhammad's use of plundering to support the Muslim empire.) That is why Al-Jihad attacked and robbed Christians in Egypt, and it is the same reason Al-Qaeda called Muslims to attack and rob Americans.

Implementing the Fatwa

On August 7, 1998 (the same year the fatwa was released), Al-Qaeda bombed the U.S. embassies in Kenya and Tanzania, killing more than two hundred people. The U.S. response was weak: on August 20, 1998, President Bill Clinton launched two cruise missiles against suspected terrorist sites in Sudan. Al-Qaeda laughed at the Clinton administration for using multimillion-dollar missiles to blow up ten-dollar tents.

Later, on October 12, 2000, Al-Qaeda tried to sink one of America's largest Navy ships, the USS *Cole*, as it sat in the harbor at Aden, Yemen. The bomb killed seventeen sailors, injured many others, and sent America's great ship home with a huge hole in the middle. This time the administration did not retaliate. It acted as if nothing happened. Now Al-Qaeda perceived a message of weakness from the United States, and bin Laden got the green light to do bigger and worse—attacking on U.S. soil for the first time since the 1993 bombing of the World Trade Centers. On September 11, 2001, his plan was put into action as four planes were hijacked. This act resulted in the collapse of the Twin Towers of the World Trade Centers in New York City, damage to the Pentagon in northern Virginia, and the crash landing of United Flight 93 in Pennsylvania, not to mention the deaths of everyone on board the four planes.

Now bin Laden had the United States' attention. A new document appeared on the Internet in Arabic in November 2002, titled "Letter to America."

Bin Laden's Letter to America—2002

Some have questioned whether this four-thousand-word document was written by bin Laden himself. In my opinion, if the letter was not written by bin Laden himself, it was certainly authorized by him. It focuses on the specific relationship between the United States and Al-Qaeda, so it will not become an enduring foundation for Islamic philosophy. But the important thing is that the letter reveals the mindset of Al-Qaeda now.[15]

The letter promised to answer the following questions:

1. Why are we fighting and opposing you?

2. What are we calling you to do, and what do we want from you?

Shouldn't the West know the answers to these questions? And who better to answer these questions than the radicals themselves!

Why Al-Qaeda fights

Just as in 1998, Al-Qaeda claimed that they are attacking the United States because the United States attacked Islam first.

What Al-Qaeda wants

People of the West do everything they can to avoid the appearance of fighting Islamic faith, but Al-Qaeda does the opposite. The letter stated that their first goal was to call the United States to convert to Islam. "The first thing we are calling you to is Islam," the letter stated. "It is to this religion that we call you, the seal of all previous religions."

Second, Al-Qaeda wants the United States to submit to Islamic law by putting an end to:

- Immorality
- Usury (charging interest)
- Intoxicants
- Gambling
- Allowing women to "serve passengers, visitors, and strangers"
- Sexual freedom

Third, Al-Qaeda calls for political changes regarding issues such as:

- Allowing Arab countries to keep weapons of mass destruction

- Prosecution of U.S. war criminals

- Treatment of Muslim prisoners in Guantánamo

- Support of Israel

- Support for secular governments, such as the Indians in Kashmir, the Russians against the Chechens, and the Manila government against Muslims in southern Philippines

- Support for "corrupt leaders in our countries." "Do not interfere in our politics and method of education," the letter stated.

Now you see the demands that Al-Qaeda makes. They are impossible to appease. Even if the United States makes every political change they demand, there is no way that America will implement *sharia* (traditional Islamic law) and stop charging interest. So Al-Qaeda will not be satisfied, and the fight will go on.

The Effects of Al-Qaeda

Now that the questions posed in bin Laden's "Letter to America" have been addressed, let us explore how Al-Qaeda has changed the landscape of terrorism in significant ways.

Engaging the entire world in the fight against Islamic terrorism

As long as radical groups only operated in their own countries and targeted their own governments, the rest of the world was satisfied to act as observers. After 9/11, the entire world became engaged. Rather than creating chaos within the borders of a specific country, Al-Qaeda has made the entire world insecure. People all over the world wonder if they are safe to ride in a plane, get on a bus, board a train, or visit a resort. This has created anger in the entire world community against radical Islamic movements where previously there was little interest.

Division in the Islamic world

The attack of 9/11, in particular, made an incredible division in the Islamic world. Before this attack, Muslims could make a pretense of being uninvolved with what was happening between radical groups and national governments. But 9/11 forced Muslims to take a position. Some Muslims were dancing in the streets after 9/11. Others were very angry at what Al-Qaeda did. This division may actually serve a positive purpose in pushing the majority of Muslim society to condemn fundamentalist Islam rather than remaining silent.

Impact on Muslims living in the West

Radical Muslim activity previous to 9/11 had little impact on the Muslims living in the West. But since 9/11, Western Muslims feel under suspicion and victimized because of Al-Qaeda's actions.

Diverse, international membership

Previous radical groups recruited members from within national borders. Al-Qaeda seeks worldwide membership, which gives the group a wide diversity of experience. Many of bin Laden's people are survivors of the Egyptian jihad movement, the Afghanistan War, the Kashmir War, the war against Israel, and many other conflicts. These men are trained terrorists, rejected by their own governments.

The Muslim Brotherhood in Egypt had more members than Al-Qaeda, but they did not have the technology at the time to become international.

This international organization includes non-Arab members from Chechnya, Kashmir, Uzbekistan, Pakistan, Kenya, and many others, including some westerners who have joined.

Suicide bombing as a primary method

Al-Qaeda has transformed the suicide bombing from something that was used occasionally by the Muslim Brotherhood or Al-Gama'a to a primary strategy for them and other small groups.

Al-Qaeda realized that they would not be able to overthrow a government through greater force. They saw the failure of such attempts by Dr. Sariah, Shokri Moustafa, and Al-Jihad. So they developed the use of the suicide bomber as an alternative.

Lawrence Wright said in his biography of al-Zawahiri in *The New Yorker*:

> Zawahiri was a pioneer in the use of suicide bombers, which became a signature of Jihad assassinations. The strategy broke powerful religious taboos against suicide and the murder of innocents.[16]

Suicide Bombing Justified

Radicals are devoutly religious, and they would not use a strategy that they believed was against the teachings of Islam. Therefore, al-Zawahiri needed to defend suicide bombing.

In his book titled *Healing the Breasts of the Believers,* al-Zawahiri does this. I downloaded this book in Arabic from al-Zaraqawi's Web site on September 8, 2005, so you can be sure this book is guiding his group as well as other radicals around the world. When you read the book, it is rather disturbing to see the scholarly, sophisticated tone al-Zawahiri uses to justify random murder.

Let's look at the two teachings he relies on to make his case.

The Story of the Boy and the King

This is a well-known, popular story throughout the Muslim world. It has been made into a video for children in Arabic and dubbed into English as well. You can find this story in English on the Web site for the Muslim Student Association of the University of Saskatoon in Canada and in the collection of hadith online at the University of Southern California. In other words, it is not secret or obscure. But let's see how al-Zawahiri can take a story that is told to children and turn it into a justification for suicide bombing.

Muhammad himself told this story, which is quite long and entertaining. Its hero is a Muslim boy named Obaid who is being trained to be a magician in the palace of a king. The boy became famous for healing people in the name of Allah. When the boy refused to give the king credit for the healings (rather than Allah), the king commanded his courtiers to kill the boy. The king's courtiers tried to kill him two different times—by throwing him off a mountain and drowning him in the sea—but he was spared by miracles both times.

The boy finally told the king, "You are not going to kill me until I tell you the way to do it."

The king asked him, "How?"

The boy said, "Gather the people together and crucify me on a tree and take an arrow from my quiver and then say, 'In the name of Allah, the lord of this boy,' and when you do that you will kill me."

The king gathered together the people in one time and one place and crucified the boy. Then he took the arrow and said, "In the name of Allah, the lord of the boy," and he shot him in the temple, and the arrow killed him.

The people shouted, "We believe in the lord of the boy."

Then the king commanded the people to renounce their faith or they would be thrown into a pit (or ditch) filled with fire. The people refused to give up their faith and instead jumped into the pit.

The story is deemed especially powerful because it is also referenced in the Quran in Surah 85:10:

> Verily, those who put into trial the believing men and believing women (by torturing them and burning them), and then do not turn in repentance, (to Allah), then they will have the torment of Hell, and they will have the punishment of the burning Fire.

Imagine how inspirational this story is to young men who are going out to fight jihad! Al-Zawahiri took this appealing, familiar story and looked to the teachings of Ibn Taymiyyah for its meaning regarding jihad. Taymiyyah wrote:

> Based on this story, the four great Muslim imams (Malik, Shafe'e, Ibn Hanbal, Abu Hanifa) allow Muslims to confront the infidels—even when they see they might be killed—as long as their deaths can benefit Muslims and Islam. And sunnah and ijma'ah agree that the Muslim should confront the enemies even if he sees that he will be killed.[17]

In other words, al-Zawahiri wrote, "The believer can sacrifice himself for the benefit of his religion." "This killing took place for one purpose: to bring victory to the message of the boy and to prepare the way for the people to come and accept the religion of Allah. And this death was absolute victory for the revelation and the religion of this young boy." Thus, suicide missions are justified.

The second great example of sacrificing one's life for the cause of Islam comes from an incident from the life of Muhammad that was observed by his companions.

The Poor Man Who Took Up the Sword

As radical groups recruit members, they often quote Muhammad's famous saying: "The gates of Paradise are under the shadow of the swords." But there is more to the story than just this slogan. Islamic history records:

> While facing the enemy, the Messenger of Allah (may peace be upon him) said: Surely, the gates of Paradise are under the shadows of the swords. A man in a shabby condition got up and said; Abu Musa, did you hear the Messenger of Allah (may peace be upon him) say this? He said: Yes. (The narrator said): He returned to his friends and said: I greet you (a farewell greeting). Then he broke the sheath of his sword, threw it away, advanced with his (naked) sword towards the enemy and fought (them) with it until he was slain.[18]

In this story, the man went into battle knowing that he would not come out alive. He said good-bye to his friends and broke the sheath of his sword to show his fate. The obvious implication is that he was rewarded by entrance into paradise. Al-Zawahiri used this story to say that a suicide bomber does the same thing: he goes into the fight knowing that he will not come out alive. But because he is doing it for the good of Islam, he will earn Paradise.

The Implications

Based on these evidences as well as other quotes from scholars, al-Zawahiri gave these practical reassurances and guidelines for jihad fighters:

1. The believer can sacrifice himself for the benefit of the religion.

2. The one who kills himself for the benefit of religion does not fall under the prohibition of suicide.

3. The one who fights and is killed in the cause of Allah does not fall under the prohibition of putting yourself in harm's way.

4. If you are going to be taken as a prisoner of war, it is good to fight to the death and refuse to be taken by enemies.

5. If you are captured and tortured, you are permitted to commit suicide to avoid giving up a secret to the enemy. This point is probably a direct result of al-Zawahiri's own prison experience of being tortured and giving information that led to the capture of his close friend. In his memoirs, which were written at the end of 2001, he indicated that he feared capture above all else:

   > Once the door of the cell is closed, the prisoner will wish that he had spent his entire life without a shelter rather than endure the humiliation of captivity. The toughest thing about captivity is forcing the mujahid [Islamic fighter] under the force of torture to confess about his colleagues' secrets to his enemies.[19]

Justifying Unintended Victims of Suicide Bombings

Suicide bomb missions kill indiscriminately and often affect civilians or other Muslims. Even a Muslim radical can be dissuaded by this fact. In an explanation dated March 1996, al-Zawahiri responds to the question: What if you are going to do an operation attacking people and there will be Muslims there beside your enemies?

Al-Zawahiri answered by telling a story about a battle Muhammad led personally against a Jewish village near Medina called Ta'if. He commanded the army to fire on everyone in the village—men, women, children, and the elderly. In another hadith, Muhammad had prohibited killing women and children, but here when he attacked the city of Ta'if he killed everybody inside. Al-Zawahiri wrote:

> At that time, women and children were there in the middle of the enemies, and there was no way to separate the enemies from them, so he had to kill all of them. This will give us light on the subject of killing the enemies of Islam who have Muslims in the middle of them. According to the law of Islam, it is one of the biggest sins for a Muslim to kill his Muslim brother, but if there is no way to kill the enemy without killing the Muslims in the middle of them, we should kill them and the enemies will go to hell and Muslims will go to Paradise.[20]

Reading this explanation, it's easy to understand how al-Zawahiri justified the attack on the World Trade Centers even though there were Muslims visiting or doing business in the Twin Towers that day.

Al-Zawahiri gave this rationale in his book titled *Healing the Breast of the Believers*. Even the title of the book reveals a great deal about his psyche and the mind-set of the group. The phrase comes from the following Quranic verses:

> Will you not fight a people who have violated their oaths (pagans of Makkah), and intended to expel the Messenger while they did attack you first?...Fight against them so that Allah will punish them by your hands and disgrace them and give you victory over them and *heal the breasts of a believing people*, and remove the anger of their (believers') hearts...
>
> —SURAH 9:13–15, EMPHASIS ADDED

In these verses, Allah calls for Muhammad to fight the people from his hometown of Mecca because they persecuted him, causing him to leave the city. Allah promised to help Muhammad punish and disgrace them. This victory would "heal the breasts [or chests]" of the Muslims and remove the anger from their hearts.

Al-Zawahiri applies these verses to modern times by saying that his book will tell Muslims how to defeat their enemies (which include the United States and allies, secular Muslim governments, and others) so that the wounds in the Muslim's chest (caused by the enemies) will be healed.

We could debate for a long time whether al-Zawahiri's accusations against the West are justified, but the fact is that he sees the battle this way, and he is going to fight it this way.

Use of Technology

Al-Qaeda and other groups are taking advantage of technology. They can use the Internet to spread pictures and video of terrorist activities. They can also distribute messages and training information.

They also have the benefit of international media as a way to enhance the effectiveness of a terrorist attack as the images of horror are distributed to the public.

Al-Qaeda's Strategy in Iraq

Bin Laden and al-Zawahiri took credit for pushing the Soviet Union out of Afghanistan. Now they are trying to do the same thing in a new venue—push the United States out of Iraq. Their methods are causing great suffering for the people of Iraq. For example, let's look at what Al-Qaeda did on September 14–15, 2005.

> The violence...included a bombing in a Shiite neighborhood of Baghdad that used a new tactic: luring scores of day laborers to a minivan with promises of work, and then blowing it up. At least 112 died in that blast alone, the second highest death toll from any single terrorist bombing in Iraq since the invasion.
>
> A suicide car bomb detonated next to a police convoy in Southern Baghdad, killing 16 people and wounding another 21.
>
> At least 10 American soldiers were wounded in attacks that the military said struck at least three military convoys.
>
> Bombings and other attacks [occurred] at the rate of several per hour.[21]

What does Al-Qaeda hope to achieve from these attacks?

There are three main reasons for Al-Qaeda to fight in Iraq.

1. *Fulfilling the law of Islam.* America and allies invaded Iraq, a Muslim country, and according to Islamic law, when a Muslim nation is invaded by a non-Muslim nation, every Muslim man and woman must defend the country.

2. *Staying on strategy.* In Afghanistan, America beat Al-Qaeda and almost destroyed it, and Al-Qaeda wants a new front for fighting America. The reason for Al-Qaeda's existence right now is to fight America and the West, and Iraq presents a good opportunity to do this.

3. *Resisting non-Muslim government.* Al-Qaeda does not want Iraq to succeed with a non-Islamic government. If democracy works in Iraq, then the United States may help other Muslim countries try it, and the Islamic world will move further and further away from Islamic law and government. Egyptian radicals were willing to destroy Egypt while attempting to install Islamic government, and they will not hesitate to do the same in Iraq. To the radicals, starting a civil war would be ideal.

And how does Al-Qaeda choose their targets? Let's look specifically at who was targeted those two particular days in September 2005. They were:

1. Shiite laborers
2. Iraqi police
3. American military

The American military were an obvious target, and the Iraqi police became a target because they are cooperating with Americans. It takes a little deeper analysis to understand why Shiite laborers were a target.

Al-Qaeda looked at the people of Iraq to see who would help them. They saw:

- Sunni Arabs
- Kurds
- Shiites

The Sunni Arabs were the most likely source of support. They had enjoyed power through Saddam Hussein and the Baath party for the past thirty years even though they were in the minority. Some of them thought, *If we can't bring back the Baath party, then we will settle for Islamic rule.* Al-Qaeda hoped to find support from them.

The Kurds are mostly Sunni, but they felt betrayed by the Muslim world for not helping them when they were persecuted by Saddam. They don't trust Muslim fundamentalists and they wanted a political solution, so they supported America. Al-Qaeda didn't get support from them.

The Shiites, who make up the majority in Iraq, were the biggest group oppressed by Saddam for many years. They welcomed the invaders for liberating them from a dictator, and they cooperated with America. America is the enemy, according to Al-Qaeda, so if the Shiites cooperate with America, the Shiites are the enemy, too. A famous saying from Ibn Taymiyyah is, "The tailor of my enemy is my enemy" (author's translation). So even if a person is just a civilian who is cooperating with America, he is a target.

WHAT BINDS RADICAL GROUPS TOGETHER?

We have seen the modern radical movement go through four generations of writers/leaders and finally produce Al-Qaeda and the global war on Islamic terrorism that we are experiencing. Each leader built on the foundation of those who came before, sometimes in agreement and sometimes refuting one point or another.

Yet certain principles were maintained from group to group, and these principles had the strength to draw in new generations of radicals as the old ones were imprisoned or executed. These principles did not stay within national borders. They were exported throughout the Muslim world, smuggled hand to hand in photocopies. Now, with the rise of the Computer Age, they are passed through disks and cyberspace, winning more Muslim hearts and minds.

From the Muslim Brotherhood to Al-Qaeda, these guiding principles are the same. I will call them the "Five Pillars of Radical Islamic Philosophy." They are:

1. Obey no law but Islamic law.
2. Infidels are all around.
3. Islam must rule.

4. Jihad is the only way to win.
5. Faith is the reason.

If you can grasp these five principles, you will have an excellent understanding of the mind-set of any Islamic radical who is basing his fight on his religion, not politics. The next five chapters will use the radicals' own words to explain these principles to you.

SECTION 3

THE FIVE PILLARS OF RADICAL ISLAMIC PHILOSOPHY

7

PILLAR 1: NO LAW BUT ISLAMIC LAW

There is one point that separates the radical Muslim from all others: Islamic law. Since the beginning of the modern revival of Islam, the radical leaders have been crying out for their governments to implement Islamic law.

Islamic law is the line that divides the religious terrorist from the secular terrorist. I have listed it as Pillar 1 because without it, the radicals would have no reason to condemn secular governments and declare jihad.

Islamic law is an incredibly powerful concept because it is viewed as a direct command from the Quran. Even more so, the radical scholars attached it inseparably to the worship of Allah. When you see the rigid logic that binds the radical to Islamic law, you will start to understand his deadly resolve.

Islamic Law Is Commanded in the Quran

The story of *sharia* (Islamic law) began with the life of Muhammad. After Muhammad became successful in Medina, he established a political system. Any political system must have a way to settle disputes or injustices; therefore, a method had to be developed. That method was simple: ask the prophet Muhammad.

During the life of Muhammad, many disputes were brought to him, and Muhammad made a decision one of two ways. He might receive a revelation from Allah regarding the question. This happened many times, and a good example is Surah 8.1, which begins, "They ask you (O Muhammad) about the spoils of war." The verses that follow provide Allah's rules for distributing the spoils that the

Muslim army captured in battle against infidels.

Another way was that Muhammad could make his own judgment, which every Muslim was expected to accept. However, one Muslim decided he didn't want to accept Muhammad's judgment, which led to the establishment of three of the most important concepts of Islamic law. Here's what happened.

Two men had a dispute and came to the prophet, who judged between them. The one who was condemned by the judgment said to his opponent, "I will not accept the judgment of Muhammad."

So the man said, "What do you want?"

The condemned man said, "We will go to Umar."

So they went to Umar ibn Al-Khattib. The man who got the favorable judgment told Umar, "We took a dispute to the prophet, and he made a judgment in my favor, and this man refuses to accept the judgment of the prophet."

Umar asked the man who was condemned, "Is this true?"

The man said, "Yes."

Islamic history says that Umar went back to his house and took his sword in his hand and came back and cut off the man's head.[1]

This killing was a huge problem because a Muslim killing another Muslim had already been established as a great crime in Islamic society. (See Surah 4:29.) Even though Umar was one of the community's most important leaders, he could be put to death for what he had done.

Muhammad struggled with this issue and then reported that the angel Gabriel told him:

> But no, by your Lord, they can have no Faith, until they make you (O Muhammad) judge in all disputes between them, and find in themselves no resistance against your decisions, and accept (them) with full submission.
>
> —Surah 4:65

The revelation established that the man who sought a judgment from Umar instead of Muhammad was no longer a muslim because he had refused to submit to the prophet. So Umar didn't kill a Muslim; he killed an infidel. This revelation saved Umar's life.

This hadith established three principles:

1. Allah says that Muslims must accept Muhammad's judgments.

2. Anyone who denies Muhammad's judgments is an infidel (because he "has no faith").

3. Any law not based on the Quran or the example of Muhammad defies the authority of the Quran because Surah 4:65 says "all disputes."

Surah 4:65 is quoted over and over again in the writings of radicals as they cry out for Islamic law and condemn all those who resist it as infidels. (See also Surahs 3:32, 132; 47:33.)

To Obey Is to Worship

There is another story from Muhammad's life that raises the stakes of Islamic law even higher. As a scholar of Islam, Sayyid Qutb explained it in his book *Milestones Along the Road.*

One hadith says that a Christian named Adi came to visit Muhammad.

> When he [Adi] came into the presence of the prophet, he was wearing a silver cross. The prophet was reciting the verse. "They (the People of the Book) have taken their rabbis and priests as lords other than God."
>
> Adi reports: "I said, 'They do not worship their priests.'"
>
> God's messenger replied, "Whatever their priests and rabbis call permissible, they accept as permissible; whatever they declare as forbidden, they consider as forbidden, and thus they worship them."[2]

In other words, Qutb said:

> Obedience to laws and judgments is a sort of worship. [Therefore], anyone who derives laws from a source other than God, in a way other than what He taught us through the Prophet, does not worship God alone.... And anyone who does this is considered out of this religion. It is taking some men as lords over others.[3]

Qutb concluded that Islam "has come to annihilate such practices, and it declares that all the people of the earth should become free of servitude to anyone other than God."[4]

Mawdudi, also trained in religion, expressed the same idea:

> No one has the right to become a self-appointed ruler of men and issue orders and prohibitions on his own volition and authority. To acknowledge the personal authority of a human being as the source of commands and prohibitions is tantamount to admitting him as the sharer in the Powers and Authority of God. And this is the root of all evils in the universe.[5]

So, to the radical, obedience to Islamic law is equivalent to worship and is utterly nonnegotiable. To be a Muslim you must obey Islamic law.

Islamic Law After Muhammad's Death

We have seen how Islamic law operated while Muhammad was alive, but what about after his death? And what kind of Islamic law does the radical envision for today?

Before Muhammad died (A.D. 634/A.H. 11), Islamic political authority had extended to all of the Arabian Peninsula. After his death, his successor, Abu Bakr, took over Muhammad's position of making decisions. Abu Bakr also gave legal authority to some of Muhammad's closest companions because they were eyewitnesses to Muhammad's previous decisions. These people included:

- Ali ibn Abu Talib, one of Muhammad's cousins
- Muwayz ibn Jabel
- Abu Hirara, one of Muhammad's servants and narrator of many hadith
- Aisha, Muhammad's second wife
- Abu Obayda
- Umar ibn Al-Khattib, who would become the second successor of Muhammad

First, these judges looked to the Quran to make their decisions. However, there are only about 250 verses from the Quran that gave specific behavioral instructions (out of a total of approximately six thousand verses).[6] So they often took the next step, which was to look for guidance from the life of Muhammad by talking to people who had memorized anecdotes about Muhammad's teachings and actions. (Thousands of these anecdotes were later gathered to create the books of hadith.) No matter who made the legal decisions, it was always clear that their decisions were based on the Quran or the sunnah.

Here's how the process worked. If you needed a *fatwa*, or legal decision, you could take your case to Ali ibn Abu Talib, one of the people who had authority to make decisions. If Ali did not remember any example from the Quran or the sunnah that matched your situation, he might tell you to go to Aisha. If you went to Aisha and she also did not know of a precedent for your situation, she would probably tell you to go to Abu Bakr.

If Abu Bakr did not know a precedent, then he would gather a group of the judges and present the issue to them together. It was easy to do this because all the people gathered for prayer at the same mosque five times a day. After he finished leading prayer, Abu Bakr would describe the issue to the judges and ask, "Do you remember anything?" If no one remembered an issue exactly the same, then Abu Bakr would ask them to try to remember similar issues. If there were no similar issues, then they had to make a new judgment based on the spirit of the Quran and the sunnah. This new judgment was called *ijma'ah*, which means "agreement" because the group had to be in agreement about the decision.

Ijma'ah Applies Islamic Law to Modern Times

Ijma'ah serves to apply Islamic law to new situations in modern times. *Ijma'ah* is an Arabic term referring to "a group in agreement." (See glossary.) For example, Islamic law says that during Ramadan you must fast between the first prayer of the day and the fourth prayer of the day. What if you become sick and need an IV? Will using an IV between the first and fourth prayer break your fast (requiring you to make up the fast at a later time)? There were no IVs in Muhammad's day, so there is not a Quranic revelation or sunnah regarding this matter. Therefore, a group of Islamic legal scholars made a judgment: if you take an IV, you have broken your fast.

These judgments, or *ijma'ah*, are often made by the Islamic Council for Research, which meets regularly at Al-Azhar University in Cairo, Egypt. The council serves as a clearinghouse for information, sending out a magazine describing new rulings, maintaining a Web site with information, and answering specific questions from judges and imams. However, the radicals do not always accept the opinion of this council because they consider it to be too politically correct and under the influence of the secular government of Egypt and other countries. So the radicals may reject the council's opinion in favor of independent scholars, such as:

- Sheikh Omar Abdul Rahman, the blind sheikh who is in prison for masterminding the 1993 attempt to blow up the World Trade Centers.

- Ibn Baz, the grand mufti of Saudi Arabia

- Yusuf al Qaradawi, former Al-Azhar scholar and president of the School of Islamic Law in Qatar

With properly executed *ijma'ah,* the Muslim radical says that Islamic law can provide a code of conduct for any circumstance, thus fulfilling his desire to bow to no authority other than Allah's. However, the *ijma'ah* is never permitted to contradict the Quran or the sunnah. Qutb wrote:

> If there is a clear text available from the Quran or from him [Muhammad], then that will be decisive, and there will be no room for ijtihad (using one's own judgment). If no such clear judgment is available, then the time comes of ijtihad—and that according to well-defined principles which are consistent with God's religion and not merely following opinions or desires.[7]

Now you know the three sources of Islamic law:

1. Quran (revelation from Allah)
2. Sunnah (example of Muhammad)
3. *Ijma'ah* (the informed decision of a qualified group of Muslim scholars)

What would it be like to live under Islamic law?

Living Under Islamic Law

Radical writers do a wonderful job of painting a beautiful picture of what living under Islamic law is like. Sayyid Qutb wrote:

> The sharia of God harmonizes the external behavior of man with his internal nature in an easy way. When a man makes peace with his own nature, peace and cooperation among individuals follow automatically, as they all live together under one system, which is a part of the general system of the universe.
>
> Thus, blessings fall on all mankind, as this way leads in an easy manner to the knowledge of the secrets of nature, its hidden forces, and the treasures concealed in the expanses of the universe.[8]

However, the real picture of Islamic law isn't nearly so appealing. The *Constitution of Al-Jihad* gives us a clear and chilling look at Islamic law in practice. The writers of that constitution set out to prove that the Egyptian government had rejected Islamic law by choosing six "crimes" and comparing the Egyptian law to the Islamic law. The choice of these six points was not random. Each one of them is based on the Quran or sunnah, thereby closing the door to the possibility of reinterpretation or *ijma'ah*. They give a very practical picture of the type of society an Islamic radical wants to establish.

1. Adultery

Adultery is considered a very serious crime in Islam, as evidenced by the fact that it was the first legal issue in this list. The judgment for adultery (sexual intercourse between persons who are not married to each other) comes from the Quran:

> The fornicatress and the fornicator, flog each of them with a hundred stripes. Let not pity withhold you in their case, in a punishment prescribed by Allah, if you believe in Allah and the Last Day. And let a party of the believers witness their punishment.
>
> —Surah 24:2

Furthermore, this judgment was practiced by Muhammad himself, as Al-Jihad wrote:

> In the Saheeh it mentions that the messenger of Allah (ordered to stone Ma'iz when he confessed adultery by saying "Take him

> and stone him," so he was stoned), the same he also did to the Ghamedian woman who committed adultery.

Islamic law also punishes fornication, which is sexual intercourse committed by non-married persons. The sentence is based on the sunnah and is generally considered to be flogging—a hundred lashes for a virgin.

With indignation, Al-Jihad went on to compare *sharia* to the Egyptian law for adultery and fornication.

> Article 273 of the Egyptian law of retributions states the following: "An adulteress may not be prosecuted unless her husband files a suit against her." There will be no punishment for her if she committed adultery with the full knowledge of her husband, as do the harlots and their pimps. Moreover there shall be no punishment for her if her husband would pardon and forgive her.
>
> And in article 274: "The married woman whose adultery was confirmed, shall be imprisoned for a period of time not to exceed two years, and her husband has the right to stop the sentencing."
>
> In article 277: "The married male adulterer will be punished by imprisonment for a period not to exceed six months, if he committed that adultery in the marital house…"
>
> Thus, the sentencing of Allah—by flogging and by stoning—is completely eradicated and is replaced by imprisonment for six months or two years.
>
> So, what kind of a challenge is this to Allah and to his messenger?
>
> It is enough that they have changed the law of adultery for a cause to bring down the legitimacy of the whole system.

2. Slander

Regarding slander, the Quran says:

> And those who accuse chaste women, and produce not four witnesses, flog them with eighty stripes, and reject their testimony forever, they indeed are the Fasiqun (liars, rebellious, disobedient to Allah).
>
> —Surah 24:4

Al-Jihad defined *slander* as "a false accusation of adultery or denying a relationship." As you can see from the verse quoted above, the punishment was beating with eighty stripes and permanently being forbidden to testify in court unless the accused repented and performed good deeds. This was compared to Egyptian law, which stated:

> Article 23: The slanderer will be punished by a period not to exceed two years of imprisonment and by a fine not less than twenty Egyptian pounds but not more than two hundred, or one of these punishments.

3. Religious conversion

Both Christians and Muslims in Islamic countries are aware of what are called the "laws of apostasy." If a Muslim chooses to abandon the Muslim faith, his punishment is death.

The first proof comes from the Quran, which says, "Whosoever of you turns back from his religion and dies as a disbeliever...they will be the dwellers of the Fire" (Surah 2:217).

The second proof comes from the sunnah. Al-Jihad noted:

> The prophet said, "He who changes his religion, kill him" and all the scholars have unanimously agreed that the punishment for conversion from the religion is death...[9]

Al-Jihad wanted the law of Egypt to say that any Muslim who leaves the Muslim faith must be executed. They complained that the Egyptian constitution states that the religion of the state is Islam, but "its laws are void of enforcing any punishment for conversion."

They blamed the Coptics (a Christian denomination) of Egypt for keeping the judgment of apostasy out of Egyptian law so that the Christians could convert Muslims to Christianity. Al-Jihad was disgusted that the Egyptian government kept "affirming the freedom of the Egyptian citizen in changing his religion any way he pleases."

In short, under Islamic law a Muslim does not have the freedom to reject Islam.

4. Consuming alcohol

Some westerners may be aware that the Quran forbids Muslims from drinking alcohol. This is the key verse:

> O you who believe! Intoxicants (all kinds of alcoholic drinks), and gambling, and Al-Ansab, and Al-Azlam (arrows for seeking luck

> or decision) are an abomination of Shaitan's (Satan) handiwork. So avoid (strictly all) that (abomination) in order that you may be successful.
>
> —Surah 5:90

The proof from the sunnah is:

> The messenger of Allah says "whoever drinks alcohol, then flog him."[10]

Al-Jihad condemned Egyptian law #63 (passed in 1976) regarding alcohol, which apparently was passed in an attempt to satisfy those who wanted Islamic laws regarding alcohol. The law would be considered very restrictive by Western standards, but it was completely unacceptable to Al-Jihad. The law stated:

> First: Offering to sell alcoholic drinks of all kinds is prohibited in all kinds of shops, boutiques, and public places, an exception to that are hotels, and tourist service establishments, or clubs of tourist nature.
>
> Second: Any type of advertising or promotion of alcoholic drinks is forbidden by all means.
>
> Third: Anyone arrested while clearly intoxicated in public will be sentenced to imprisonment of a period not less than two weeks, and not to exceed six months, or by fine not less than twenty pounds and not more than one hundred pounds.

You can see an important aspect of the mind-set of a Muslim radical from the way Al-Jihad responded to these laws. Halfway won't work. It didn't help that Egyptian law put some restrictions on alcohol. It had to go the whole way. It's either complete submission to Islamic law or war.

5. Robbery

Many westerners have heard it said that Islamic law requires a person who is convicted of stealing to have his hand cut off. They often wonder if this is really a requirement of Islam or a fanatical interpretation by radicals. Let's look at the proofs offered by Al-Jihad.

First, the Quran says:

> And (as for) the male thief and the female thief, cut off (from the wrist joint) their (right) hands as a recompense for that which they committed, a punishment by way of example from Allah.
>
> —Surah 5:38

Second, the sunnah confirmed:

> The prophet ordered the hand of the thief (male and female) to be cut off.[11]

Al-Jihad complained:

> As far as the Egyptian laws are concerned, they are as far from these laws as heaven is from earth. Article 317 of the law of punishments for felonies of robbery under the strict conditions would penalize its committer by jail with labor for a total period of three years.
>
> In article 318 if the robbery was committed under ordinary conditions, then its punishment would not exceed two years with labor.

According to Al-Jihad, the only acceptable punishment is to cut off the hand. Prison is not acceptable.

6. Usury

It is hard to imagine any government in modern times that would be able to sustain an economy without charging interest for the use of money over time. Islamic law, however, forbids usury, based on the words of the Quran:

> Allah will destroy Riba (usury) and will give increase for Sadaqat (deeds of charity, alms, etc.) And Allah likes not the disbelievers, sinners.
>
> —Surah 2:276

However, Al-Jihad complained that article 226 of Egyptian civil law permits "adding interest to the delayed payments of money due."

Al-Jihad's conclusion

Al-Jihad concluded that these six points were more than enough to declare the government of Egypt infidel and illegitimate.

> Isn't this enough? Isn't what we have mentioned up to here... enough?...All that is considered a combat and a direct duel with the laws of Allah and his commandments.

Enforcing Islamic Law

Al-Jihad made plans to fully implement Islamic law after they came to power. Abod Zoummar, a key leader of Al-Jihad, envisioned "callers" who would be assigned to "promote the good deeds and prohibit the shameful." If a caller discovered a person breaking Islamic law, the caller could take the following steps:

- First, meeting someone
- Second, introducing himself
- Third, prohibiting by preaching or giving advice or by fear of Allah
- Fourth, chastising by rebuking and reprimanding without using foul language
- Fifth, preventing by force, such as destroying night clubs and dumping out alcohol
- Sixth, by fear and threatening of battering
- Seventh, hitting with fists or by kicking and the like, but not using a weapon
- Eighth, if he cannot overcome alone, then he should ask for helpers who carry weapons

If you are a non-Muslim living in a Muslim country, Qutb says you will have to submit to Islamic law (even though you are not required to convert to Islam).

> But in an Islamic system there is room for all kinds of people to follow their own beliefs while obeying the laws of the country, which are themselves based on the divine authority.[12]

Mawdudi also said:

> Islamic "Jihad" does not seek to interfere with the faith, ideology, rituals of worship or social customs of the people. It allows them perfect freedom of religious belief and permits them to act according to their creed. However, Islamic "Jihad" does not recognize their right to administer State affairs according to a system which, in the view of Islam, is evil.[13]

Who would want to live in this kind of society? Nobody but a radical Muslim. That's why Muslim governments won't accept Islamic law. The average Muslim has no desire to live like this.

Who Met the Standard?

Was there any country that met the standards of the Islamic radicals in the 1970s? The answer is, no, not one. The radicals condemned them all.

> All the regimes, as well as all the Islamic countries, have chosen methods, regulations, and legislations other than the book or the sunnah, thus forsaking Allah, while assigning themselves as gods.[14]

Radicals particularly condemned democracy for giving the people the power to make law. As Dr. Sariah explained:

> Democracy, for example, has become a way of life, but it is contrary to Islam. In democracy the people have the legal right in legislation to permit what they permit and prohibit what they prohibit, like permitting sodomy as has happened in England lately, or to permit group marriages as has happened in Sweden. In Islam, however, the people have no authority in permitting the prohibited or prohibiting the permitted, even if the whole populace agreed to it. Therefore, combining Islam and democracy is like combining Islam and Judaism, since one cannot be a Jew and a Muslim at the same time, he cannot be a Muslim and democratic as well.[15]

Where Is *Sharia* Practiced Today?

As of 2005 there were fifty-six countries in the Muslim World League. Although they would all claim to base their legal system on *sharia,* in reality, almost none of them do it fully. The only governments fully implementing *sharia* right now are in Iran and Saudi Arabia. (Afghanistan under Taliban rule would have also been included in this short list.) Two other countries that are close to practicing *sharia* completely are Pakistan and the Maldive Islands, off the southwest coast of India.

The foremost school for studying Islamic law is Al-Azhar in Cairo, but there are also major schools in Saudi Arabia, Algeria, India, and Pakistan. Students of Islamic law first learn the rulings of the Quran and sunnah. Then they study books written by Islamic scholars throughout Islamic history, which record fatwas and explain them. Some of the key books are:

- *Fiqh-us-Sunnah* by Sayyid Sabiq (1915–2000). Sabiq wrote this multi-volume set in the 1940s when he was only thirty years old at the request of Hasan al-Banna, the founder of the Muslim Brotherhood. It was translated into English in the early 1990s and is available online at http://www.usc.edu/dept/MSA/law/fiqhussunnah/fusintro.html.

- *Fatawa al Cobra* [The Great Legal Opinions] by Ibn Taymiyyah (1268–1328)

- *Al Halal wal Haram* [Enjoining Right, Forbidding Wrong] by Ibn Taymiyyah (1268–1328)

Although governments have not fully adopted *sharia,* individuals and groups strive to follow it. They rely on what they know of Quran and sunnah as well as the teachings of their leaders or imams. For Muslims in the West, some Islamic groups produce books in English that describe the basics of *sharia.*

It Couldn't Happen Here!

Although it is very difficult to imagine *sharia* as the law of a Western nation, we may get to see parts of *sharia* implemented very close to home—in Canada! The Religion Report radio program reported:

> In 2003, an organisation called the Islamic Institute of Civil Justice was established in Ontario to serve as an arbitration body for Ontario's Muslim communities. The Institute was set up to use principles of Islamic law to arbitrate on matters of family and inheritance, and Muslims would be required to use it rather than the secular courts to settle disputes, as a testament of their faith....
>
> Since then, alarm bells have been ringing all over Canada, particularly on the part of Muslim women's groups, who say that Islamic law doesn't view women as equal to men, and that therefore it can't provide justice on issues of divorce, or child custody or the division of property.[16]

In other words, Muslims in Canada can choose to have legal matters regarding family life decided by arbitration based on *sharia*. This is a voluntary choice, yet in reality, people in the Muslim community will feel significant pressure to accept this arbitration in order to appear to be good Muslims.

This arbitration could not be applied to criminal law, and it could not produce a punishment that is inconsistent with Canadian law. This leads some women to ask, "If Islamic law has to be watered down to be consistent with Canadian law, why don't we just follow Canadian law?"

It couldn't happen in the West? Let's watch and see how far *sharia* makes it in Canada.

Conclusion

For a radical, there is no negotiation concerning Islamic law. They will work—and die, if necessary—to fulfill every single judgment. Why? Because they want to prove to Allah and his prophet, to themselves, and to society that they are true followers of the prophet. They are sincere, not playing a game with their faith. They are not willing to lose their eternity by compromising the law in their lives. In their mind's eye, they are the only group to uphold the truth in a world of infidels.

8

PILLAR 2: INFIDELS ARE ALL AROUND

The radical sees himself as surrounded by infidels who are hostile to him and his message of faith. All the key radical writers put great energy into arguing that nearly all societies are infidel—both those who call themselves Muslims and the others. The writers repeatedly elaborate on the following three themes:

1. Denying Islamic law makes you an infidel.
2. Accepting part of Islam while refusing another part makes you an infidel.
3. Infidel governments must be destroyed.

Let's look at these themes in detail.

Denying Islamic Law

To be a Muslim you must submit to Islamic law, the radicals say. They appeal to three key Quranic verses, which you will remember from Pillar 1 of radical philosophy. The Quran says:

> But no, by your Lord, they can have no Faith, until they make you (O Muhammad) judge in all disputes between them, and find in themselves no resistance against your decisions, and accept (them) with full submission.
>
> —Surah 4:65

> If any do fail to judge by (the light of) what Allah has revealed, they are (no better than) Unbelievers.
>
> —Surah 5:44, Ali translation

> Say: "Obey Allah and His Messenger": but if they turn back [away from Islam], Allah does not love those who reject Faith.
>
> —Surah 3:32, Ali translation

Radicals use these verses to sweepingly condemn nearly the whole world as infidel.

In reference to infidels, Qutb liked to use a classical Arabic term, *jahiliyyah* [jah hi LEE yuh], which is used in the Quran to refer to the society that existed in ignorance of Allah. The word conveys a sense of ignorance, savagery, and willful sinfulness.

Qutb wrote:

> A *jahili* society [is one] which does not dedicate itself to submission to God alone, in its beliefs and ideas in its observances of worship, and in its legal regulations.[1]

According to this definition, all the societies existing in the world today are *jahili.*

This is the simple, factual way to say it. But some radicals liked to make the point more dramatically. Dr. Sariah wrote, for example:

> Everyone who objects to the judgments of Islam or is not satisfied with them is an infidel; therefore, all those who have written anything against the legal limits of Islam, by labeling the cutting of the hand of the thief or stoning the adulterer, as regression or as degenerative and the likes of these descriptions, and those who demand the annulment of punishment by execution, and object to the prohibition of alcohol, or anything that might be considered an objection to the judgments of Allah, are straight infidels, whose blood is spilled, his wife would be divorced from him, and he will not be prayed over, and will not be buried in the graves of the Muslims, and he does not inherit, nor is allowed to leave an inheritance.[2]

Accepting Some/Rejecting Some

The radicals see Islam as an all-or-nothing faith. They do not have any flexibility on any part of Islamic law. They defend their position by quoting two famous stories from Islamic teaching.

1. Illegally charging usury

A group of Muslims wanted to keep charging interest (usury) for loans, even though the Quran prohibited it. Ibn Taymiyyah, also known as the Sheikh of Islam, explained:

> The people of Taif had accepted Islam, and prayed and fasted, but they were still dealing with usury. Allah then brought down this verse and ordered the believers through it to leave what remained of the usury: "The Exalted said 'O ye who believe! Fear Allah, and give up what remains of your demand for usury, if ye are indeed believers. If ye do it not, Take notice of war from Allah and His Messenger'" (Surah 2:278).
>
> Knowing that usury is the last of the things forbidden in the Quran, and those who would practice it are to be fought against, how much more must be fought those who did not abstain from other things forbidden, which are of a higher and more restricted stance.[3]

In other words, if Allah required Muhammad to go to war against those who would not give up usury (charging interest), how much more must Muslims fight those leaders who abandon a great part of the teachings of Islam?[4]

The Quran says:

> Surely those who disbelieve in Allah and His apostles and (those who) desire to make a distinction between Allah and His apostles and say: We believe in some and disbelieve in others, and desire to take a course between (this and) that. These it is that are truly the unbelievers, and we have prepared for the unbelievers a disgraceful chastisement.
>
> —Surah 4:150–151, Shakir Translation

For example, if you keep up prayer five times a day (as the Quran commands) but take Christians and Jews for friends (as the Quran forbids), then you are an infidel for believing some and rejecting some.

2. Refusing to pay the tax

When Abu Bakr took charge after Muhammad's death, a group of new Muslim converts refused to pay the tax any longer. Abu Bakr sent his best general to fight them, and he killed eighty thousand people in three bloody months. Because Abu Bakr was the closest companion to Muhammad, this proves to the radicals that there must be no tolerance of partial obedience.

For example, the *Constitution of Al-Jihad* says:

> Those who abstained from paying the alms at the time of Abu Bakr did so not because they denied its prerequisite but because of their stinginess, and they were fought by the comrades of the prophets. Thus it became known that *any sect that has a concern and abstains from abiding by the law of Islam will be fought, even if they had acknowledged it [the law of Islam].*[5]

Al-Jihad then applied the words of Ibn Taymiyyah:

> Any group that has associated itself to Islam, and at the same time has abstained from practicing some of its apparent continued precepts, *must be fought by agreement of all Muslims,* until the whole religion is to Allah (emphasis added).[6]

Faraj also pointed to Abu Bakr's decision as a clear directive that "a sect must be fought if they abandon a few of the continuous and apparent observances, even if they still utter the two declarations but refrained from praying, or paying the poor-dues [tax or *zakat*], or fasting the month of Ramadan, or taking a pilgrimage."[7]

Islam is a comprehensive unit, wrote Dr. Sariah; if one believes some of it and neglects the rest he becomes an infidel.[8]

Infidel Governments Must Be Destroyed

If you are a Muslim and your government refuses to apply all of Islamic law, then you are obligated to overthrow your government, say the radicals. Qutb wrote:

> The position of Islam in relations to all these *jahili* societies can be described in one sentence: it considers all these societies unIslamic and illegal.[9]

> *Jahaliyyah* is evil and corrupt, whether it be of the ancient or modern variety.[10]

> The foremost duty of Islam in this world is to depose *Jahiliyyah* from the leadership of man, and to take the leadership into its own hands and enforce the particular way of life which is its permanent feature.[11]

Radical Muslim scholars compare their situation to the time when the Mongols conquered the Muslim Empire. In a short time, the Mongols accepted Islam, but they also retained their own legal system. This piece of history yielded a rich trove of fatwas, written by an Islamic scholar known as Ibn Taymiyyah, for radicals to use against their enemies. The radicals quote from many scholars, but Ibn Taymiyyah always has a special place.

Ibn Taymiyyah condemned the Mongols as infidel for not accepting Islamic law and declared that Muslims had an obligation to overthrow their government.[12]

Therefore, 725 years later, Al-Jihad declared:

> Those tyrants who govern the countries of Islam with other than the commandments of Islam, must be revolted against and fought, and Muslims are in no way to... concede to their atheism and their sinfulness no matter how much they claim that they will one day adopt the religious law.[13]

House of Peace/House of War

The terms *House of Peace* and *House of War* are often used in radical writings. These terms do not come directly from the Quran or hadith, but the early scholars of Islam created these terms in order to describe the environment of a place where a Muslim may be living. For example, Mecca during the time of Muhammad's weakness and persecution would have been a house of war (*Dar-ul-Harb*). As a result, after he was prepared, Muhammad declared war on Mecca and established Islamic authority there. Medina, when it was governed and ruled by Muslims, would be considered a house of peace (*Dar-ul-Islam*).

Abu Hanifa, one of the founders of the four Muslim legal schools, had a moderate standard for these two terms. He said the most important issue is the security of Muslims. If Muslims are in a secure place, it is *Dar-ul-Islam*; if not, then they are in *Dar-ul-Harb*. By these standards, a nation where Islam could be practiced freely (such as the United States or England) would be considered *Dar-ul-Islam*. However, another group of Muslim scholars reject this definition. They say that *Dar-ul-Harb* is any place not ruled by Islam and submitting to Islamic law.[14]

Sayyid Qutb popularized the strict interpretation in his most influential book, *Milestones Along the Road*. Qutb declared:

1. *Dar-ul-Islam* is that place where the Islamic state is established and the *sharia* is the authority and God's limits are observed and where all the Muslims administer the affairs of the state with mutual consultation.

2. The rest of the world is the home of hostility (*Dar-ul-Harb*). A Muslim can have only two possible relations with *Dar-ul-Harb*: peace with a contractual agreement or war. A country with which there is a treaty will not be considered the home of Islam.[15]

A Muslim must only declare loyalty to *Dar-ul-Islam*, not to a particular nationality. Qutb wrote:

> A Muslim has no country except that part of the earth where the Sharia of God is established...; a Muslim has no nationality except his belief...; a Muslim has no relatives except those who share the belief in God.[16]

A committed Muslim will have only one defining characteristic—his faith. All other identity not based in his faith is irrelevant, including lineage, race, nationality, and family. These relationships were from the time of ignorance before Islam, says the radical. Qutb stated this concept simply at times, or in poetic, majestic language, such as:

> Islam freed all humanity from the ties of earth, so that they might soar toward the skies and freed them from the chains of blood relationship—the biological chains—so that they might rise above the angels.[17]

The Danger of Jews and Christians

It goes without saying that Jews and Christians are infidels. But the Quran teaches the radical that Jews and Christians also deserve additional suspicion as well. The radicals honestly believe that Jews and Christians (as embodied by the West) want to destroy the Islamic faith. The Quran says:

> Many of the followers of the Book wish that they could turn you back into unbelievers after your faith, out of envy from themselves, (even) after the truth has become manifest to them; but pardon and forgive, so that Allah should bring about His command; surely Allah has power over all things.
>
> —Surah 2:109, Shakir Translation

> And the Jews will not be pleased with you, nor the Christians until you follow their religion. Say: Surely Allah's guidance, that is the (true) guidance. And if you follow their desires after the knowledge that has come to you, you shall have no guardian from Allah, nor any helper.
>
> —Surah 2:120, Shakir Translation

> O you who believe! if you obey a party from among those who have been given the Book, they will turn you back as unbelievers after you have believed.
>
> —Surah 3:100, Shakir Translation

With these teachings in the Quran, it is little wonder that Muslims are suspicious of every action from the West. They believe the West is entirely Christian, and, therefore, every move is scrutinized for a religious motive. Qutb commented:

> After this warning to the Muslims from God concerning the ultimate designs of the Jews and the Christians, it would be extremely shortsighted of us to fall into the illusion that when the Jews and Christians discuss Islamic beliefs or Islamic history, or when they make proposals concerning Muslim society or Muslim politics or economics, they will be doing it with good intentions, or with the welfare of the Muslims at heart, or in order to seek guidance and light.[18]

> The enmity toward Islam [from the West] is especially pronounced and many times is the result of a well-thought-out scheme, the object of which is first to shake the foundations of Islamic beliefs and then gradually to demolish the structure of Muslim society.[19]

Sayyid Qutb did not write these words simply because he disliked America. He was applying the words of the Quran.

Conclusion

In conclusion, the radical is convinced that he is surrounded by infidels who must be fought to preserve Islam. His ultimate goal is to restore the caliphate: "Islam must rule." This is the focus of the third pillar, which you will read next.

9

PILLAR 3: ISLAM MUST RULE

Westerners see the news about bombings and terrorism in Muslim nations and in the West. Many times they throw up their hands in frustration and ask, "What do these people want? What are they trying to get?"

The answer is this: these terrorists want the caliphate back, and they ultimately want the caliphate to have authority over the entire world. Where do they get these ideas? Are they misrepresenting Islam, or are they trying to finish what Muhammad started?

The Fall of the Caliphate

Muslims in general are very proud of the history of the caliphate in Islam. For thirteen centuries, the caliphate united Muslim lands both spiritually and politically. The *Constitution of Al-Jihad* described the end of the caliphate bitterly:

> In the year 1924 the wicked and the spiteful Kamal Ataturk [leader of Turkey] declared the total fall of the Islamic caliphate, and eventually he separated Turkey from the Islamic world.[1]

Turkey's action to end the caliphate caused great emotional pain to Muslim individuals. To make a clumsy analogy, it would be something like the nation of Italy outlawing the pope and doing away with the Vatican.

Listen to the despair and disbelief in the way Al-Jihad described the fall:

> Deleting the caliphate was the biggest crime during the term of this government against the state, and the most horrific crime in the history of Islam against Islam. What evil did these infidels think they were avoiding by ending the caliphate... and what good were they thinking will come out of this deed?[2]

A few words of a poem in the text will further clarify the feeling:

> Sister of Andalucia peace be upon you
> The caliphate and Islam have fallen off of you
> The crescent have disappeared from the sky, I wish
> The sky had disappeared instead, and darkness filled the world...[3]

"If only the caliphate would be restored, all our problems would melt away," says the radical. "We would return to the glory days of Islam."

Obedience to Allah

The radical sees the establishment of the caliphate as a matter of submission to Allah. The key verse always quoted by the radicals is:

> O Dawud (David)! Verily! We have placed you as a successor on earth; so judge you between men in truth (and justice)...
>
> —Surah 38:26

In Arabic, the word for *successor* is *caliph*. So in this verse Allah tells David that he is a *caliph* on the earth, which for the Muslim establishes the concept of the caliphate.

The Quran says elsewhere that the caliphate is promised to the believers (Muslims):

> Allah has promised those among you who believe and do righteous good deeds, that He will certainly grant them succession to (the present rulers) in the land, as He granted it to those before them...
>
> —Surah 24:55

The verse goes on to describe the characteristics of the caliphate—that it will make it easy for Muslims to practice their religion and will give them security in place of fear.

> He will grant them the authority to practise their religion which He has chosen for them (i.e. Islam). And He will surely give them in exchange a safe security after their fear (provided) they (believers) worship Me.

Radical preachers love to quote this verse in their sermons. However, the concept of the caliphate is not merely based on proof-texting. It is established through the example of Muhammad himself.

Destroy Infidel Governments

Islam is not merely belief, points out Qutb. You can't just preach about it. It is a way of life that must take shape as a system of authority on earth, just as it did during the life of Muhammad. In short, Islam is a religion and a state. Muhammad sought to persuade by preaching during the first thirteen years after his revelation. In contrast, after he emigrated from Mecca to Medina, he set up a political government, established laws, and established Islam as a system of belief that covers every aspect of life. Qutb reasoned that no political system on earth will allow Islam to function completely; therefore, all other systems must be destroyed.

> Other societies do not give it [Islam] any opportunity to organize its followers according to its own method, and hence it is the duty of Islam to annihilate all such systems, as they are obstacles in the way of universal freedom. Only in this manner can the way of life be wholly dedicated to God.[4]

Mawdudi wrote bluntly:

> Islam wishes to destroy all States and Governments anywhere on the face of the earth which are opposed to the ideology and programme of Islam regardless of the country or the Nation which rules it.[5]

Strategy to Establish Global Islamic Authority

The radical plans to restore the caliphate by accomplishing three goals.

1. Establish Islamic states.

2. Join these states together under the caliphate.

3. Use the caliphate to submit the entire world to Islamic authority.

Radicals are frustrated that they have been unable to successfully accomplish step 1 thus far, and they blame the United States. In the 2002 Letter to America Al-Qaeda complains:

> Under your [the United States'] supervision, consent and orders, the governments of our countries which act as your agents attack us on a daily basis; these governments prevent us from establishing the Islamic sharia…

Al-Qaeda threatens to attack the United States again if she does not withdraw support of secular Muslim governments:

> We call upon you to end your support of the corrupt leaders in our countries. Do not interfere in our politics and method of education. Leave us alone, or else expect us in New York and Washington.

If Al-Qaeda did succeed at establishing Islamic governments in several nations, then they would work to put these nations under the umbrella of a caliphate again so that they could act as one to expand the Islamic empire again, as in the glory days of the Ottoman Empire (which you will read about later in this book). The ultimate goal would be to put the entire world under Islamic authority and in obedience to Islamic law.

Nationality Means Nothing

To a committed radical who is fighting for his faith, the caliphate means everything and nationality means nothing. His nationality is now belief in Islam. As Qutb wrote:

> The people who are really chosen by God are the Muslim community which has gathered under God's banner without regard to differences of races, nations, colors and countries.
>
> > "You are the best community raised for the good of mankind. You enjoin what is good and forbid what is evil, and you believe in God." (3:110)

> Nationalism here is belief, homeland here is *Dar-ul-Islam*, the ruler here is God, and the constitution here is the Qur'an.[6]

Radicals love to use the slogan, "Our constitution is the Quran." A religious radical is not fighting for Iraq, Syria, or Palestine. He is fighting to set up the House of Islam where Allah rules and the constitution is the Quran.

Conclusion

Radicals are not crazy. They are intelligent, logical people who are following the teachings of their faith all the way—where most people never want to go. So here's what we've established about their mind-set thus far:

1. There can be no law but Islamic law.
2. Infidels who reject Islamic law are all around.
3. The caliphate must be restored to give Muslims the freedom to practice their faith.

The next logical step is, how can the caliphate be restored? Faraj explained the logic simply:

1. In order to establish the caliphate there needs to be an Islamic state.
2. If the establishment of the state cannot be accomplished without going to war, then war is also a duty.

The simple answer is jihad. The radical has no difficulty finding teaching about the duty of jihad in the Quran, as you will see in the next chapter.

10

PILLAR 4: JIHAD IS THE ONLY WAY TO WIN

The Islamic radical is a fundamentalist—he wants to practice Islam the way Muhammad practiced Islam. So his definition of jihad is based on Muhammad's—both in word and by example.

Readers in modern times may struggle to reconcile the different teachings in the Quran regarding tolerance toward non-Muslims, but the first Muslim community had no such difficulty because they experienced that jihad was revealed in stages.

Qutb described the following stages:

1. For thirteen years after the beginning of his Messengership, Muhammad called people to God through preaching, without fighting or *Jizyah* (tax). He was commanded to restrain himself and to practice patience and forbearance.

2. Next, he was commanded to emigrate to Medina, and permission was later given to fight.

3. Then he was commanded to fight those who fought him and to restrain himself from those who did not make war with him.

4. Later he was commanded to fight the polytheists until God's religion was fully established.[1]

To put it simply, when the Quran speaks of living in humility and submission, it was a temporary condition. Stage 1 is past, and Muslim community is in stage 4 permanently.

Those who speak against jihad "speak clumsily and mix up the various stages," complained Qutb. "They regard every verse of the Qur'an as if it were the final principle of this religion."[2]

Progressive Revelation (Abrogation)

The stages of jihad will become even clearer when you understand a principle of Quranic interpretation known as *nasikh*. *Nasikh* is the idea that revelation in the Quran is progressive. In other words, when there is a contradiction, newer revelations cancel out, or abrogate, older revelations. For example, drinking alcohol was first permitted any time, then permitted any time except during prayer, and finally forbidden at all times. The direction for prayer was originally Jerusalem, and then it changed to Mecca.

In the same way, the revelations about jihad abrogated the earlier verses that were about tolerance, such as Surah 2:109:

> Quite a number of the People of the Book wish they could turn you (people) back to infidelity after you have believed...but forgive and overlook...
>
> —Ali translation

This verse sounds like tolerance embodied, but it was canceled out by a newer revelation known as the "verse of the sword."

> So when the sacred months have passed away, then slay the idolaters wherever you find them, and take them captives and besiege them and lie in wait for them in every ambush.
>
> —Surah 9:5, Shakir Translation

Al-Jihad quoted an explanation of this verse from the classic scholar Al-Kalbi:

> This indicates an abrogation to all that was previously given to the infidels of peace treaties, and pardon certificates, and avoiding them or being patient with the harm they cause. And the order to engage them in battle here is clear for all times and everywhere.

> So in the Quran there are 114 verses from 54 Chapters (Sura), which all have been abrogated by his words: "slay the idolaters wherever you find them" and "fighting is enjoined on you."[3]

You can still read the abrogated verses in the Quran, but they are no longer applicable as a guide for living.

The Quran contains a tremendous amount of teaching about jihad. In fact, I estimate that 60 percent of the Quran is related to the concept of jihad. Following are some examples of the verses that radicals like to quote.

Key Verses About Jihad From the Quran

Rescue the oppressed

Radicals believe non-Muslims who oppress them cause all their problems. Therefore, they readily identify with verses such as these:

> And what is wrong with you that you fight not in the Cause of Allah, and for those weak, ill-treated and oppressed among men, women, and children, whose cry is: "Our Lord! Rescue us from this town whose people are oppressors; and raise for us from You one who will protect, and raise for us from You one who will help."
>
> —Surah 4:75

Al-Jihad declared:

> It has been imposed upon the Muslims the preparation of a strong army raising the banner of unification and going out in the name of Allah, to champion the religion of Allah, to soothe the wounds of the nation of Islam, and to repel the raping enemies who have plundered the land, and ransacked its wealth, and humiliated its people.
>
> It has become compulsory upon Muslims today to fight and go to war to save the thousands of prisoners and the millions of weakened masses who are vulnerable and helpless.[4]

Fight with your wealth and your lives

The Quran tells Muslims:

> March forth, whether you are light (being healthy, young and wealthy) or heavy (being ill, old and poor), strive hard with your

> wealth and your lives in the Cause of Allah. This is better for you, if you but knew.
>
> —Surah 9:41

Punishment for neglecting jihad

The Quran condemned Muslims who avoided the duty of jihad.

> O you who believe! What (excuse) have you that when it is said to you: Go forth in Allah's way, you should incline heavily to earth; are you contented with this world's life instead of the hereafter? But the provision of this world's life compared with the hereafter is but little. If you do not go forth, He will chastise you with a painful chastisement and bring in your place a people other than you, and you will do Him no harm; and Allah has power over all things.
>
> —Surah 9:38–39, Shakir Translation

This verse was revealed while Muhammad was preparing his people to go fight in the Campaign of Tabuk. Some Muslims hesitated to go and fight, so this verse warned them that Allah would punish the ones who refused to go and replace them with better people.

Prepare for war

> And We brought forth iron wherein is mighty power (in matters of war), as well as many benefits for mankind, that Allah may test who it is that will help Him (His religion) and His Messengers in the unseen.
>
> —Surah 57:25

This verse praises iron for its benefit in battle. Religious radicals are eager to use the best technology to fight jihad. *The Noble Quran*, published by King Fahd of Saudi Arabia, presents this bold translation and explanation of Surah 8:60:

> And make ready against them all you can of power, including steeds of war (tanks, planes, missiles, artillery) to threaten the enemy of Allah and your enemy, and others besides whom, you may not know but whom Allah does know. And whatever you shall spend in the Cause of Allah shall be repaid unto you, and you shall not be treated unjustly.

The Sheikh Abu Bakr Al-Jazeeri explained this passage in practical and severe terms:

> Muslims must prepare weapons and gather material and military equipment, and train men to the different arts of war, not to repel the attacks of the enemies only but to also enable them to conduct raids to the cause of Allah, and uplift His word, and to spread justice and mercy and good on earth.
>
> Also the military draft should be enforced in the Islamic countries so that every man would be prepared for the military service...
>
> Muslims must also establish factories to produce all kinds of weapons in the world with the latest innovations, even if this means that they have to sacrifice eating or drinking or clothing or dwelling except what is necessary, something which would place them rightfully in performing their duties for war to the fullest, otherwise they are guilty and would be subjected to the wrath of Allah now and in eternity.[5]

In battle, smite the necks

The world was horrified by videotapes of beheadings in Iraq. People wondered why religious radicals would commit this grisly act. The answer is in the Quran:

> Therefore, when you meet the Unbelievers (in fight), smite at their necks; at length, when you have thoroughly subdued them, bind a bond firmly (on them)...
>
> —Surah 47:4, Ali translation

Rewards for jihad

In radical writings, the authors rarely mention rewards for jihad or martyrdom because it is such a widely accepted and understood principle. There is no need to justify it. The reward for being killed in jihad is guaranteed entrance to paradise, as the Quran states:

> Let those (believers) who sell the life of this world for the Hereafter fight in the Cause of Allah, and whoso fights in the Cause of Allah, and is killed or gets victory, We shall bestow on him a great reward.
>
> —Surah 4:74

MUHAMMAD'S TEACHINGS ABOUT JIHAD

In addition to the words of the Quran, we also have Muhammad's example as recorded in hadith. Radicals like to quote a declaration Muhammad made while he was still living in Mecca:

> Listen people of Quraysh, by the one who has the soul of Muhammad in his hand, I have come to you as a slaughterer.[6]

Al-Jihad said of this quote:

> The community took his word seriously enough...to where the toughest of them would meet him with the best words there are.... So by saying, "I have come to you as a slaughterer" he paved the straight way which contains no argument and no wheedling with the leaders of disbelief and the patrons of infidelity.[7]

Later Muhammad would make good on his words when he came with an army of Muslims ten thousand strong and defeated Mecca.

In the last recorded sermon before his death, Muhammad confirmed the place of the sword in Islam. Radicals like to quote him saying:

> I descended by Allah with the sword in my hand, and my wealth will come from the shadow of my sword. And the one who will disagree with me will be humiliated and persecuted.[8]

MODERATE MUSLIMS CHALLENGE JIHAD

Moderate Muslims who do not want to fight a physical jihad need to find alternative explanations for the teachings about jihad in the Quran and hadith. However, religious radicals always push back against any moderate teachings that say jihad is not primarily a physical fight. Here are three examples.

GREATER JIHAD AND LESSER JIHAD

Moderate Muslims often say that the highest meaning of jihad is a spiritual struggle within oneself to follow the teachings of Islam. Where do they get this idea? They point to a story recorded in the hadith:

> Muhammad was returning from a battle when he told one of his friends, "We are returning from the little jihad to the great jihad."

> His friend asked him, "O prophet of Allah, what do you mean by the small battle and the great battle?"
>
> Muhammad replied, "The small battle is the battle we just came from where we were fighting the enemies of Islam. The great battle is the spiritual struggle of the Muslim life."[9]

In other words, the story says that the lesser jihad was the physical battle and the greater jihad was the spiritual battle within. This phrase "greater jihad" is used often by liberal Muslims.

There are some challenges to this hadith that you should know about.

1. Most importantly, it is inconsistent with the other teachings of Muhammad and the Quran. The Quran gives Muslims many guidelines for living, but the Quran never describes the struggle to follow these guidelines as "jihad."

2. The documentation that links this story to the actual life of Muhammad is weak. Orthodox Muslim scholars believe that Muhammad never said this. Sheikh al-Elbeni, the most respected scholar of hadith in the world, lists this as a weak hadith, even though it comes from otherwise reliable historians. Ibn Al Qayyem blasted the story as an "invented statement. And those who invented it aimed at nothing except to belittle the importance of the sword."[10]

Categories of jihad

Some moderates say that jihad is divided into three categories (per Islamic scholar, Imam Ibn Al-Qayyim):

1. Jihad of the soul
2. Jihad against Satan
3. Jihad against the infidels and hypocrites

They say jihad of the soul and jihad against Satan must be completed before starting jihad against infidels and hypocrites. Faraj scathingly responded:

> This dedication by some shows total ignorance and/or total cowardice, because Ibn Al-Qayyim divided jihad into categories, not stages. Otherwise we would have to stop struggling against Satan until we have finished the struggle of the soul. The fact is that all three of these categories go hand in hand in a straight line.[11]

Self-defense

Moderates often argue that jihad was only used to defend the homeland of Islam.

Qutb pointed out that the goal of the first caliphs was to spread Islam as far as they possibly could, which included offensives against Roman and Persian powers whether they were a threat or not. The purpose of jihad was to make way for the preaching of Islam, unhindered by an infidel government, says Qutb.[12] Whether it is true or not, Qutb insisted that any non-Muslim government will hinder the teaching of Islam.

> A jahiliyyah system will put obstacles in the way of preaching Islam.[13]

> Political powers... prevent people from listening to the preaching and accepting the belief if they wish to do so.[14]

Three Important Concepts

In addition to refuting arguments against physical jihad, radical writers also clarified other concepts about how to practice jihad. Below are three of the most important ones.

1. Jihad is an individual duty, not a corporate duty.

Radicals seek to prove that jihad is obligatory to every Muslim. There are two types of duties in Islam—individual and corporate. Individual duties, such as prayer, fasting, and giving alms, are required of every Muslim. Corporate duties, on the other hand, must be fulfilled by some, but not all, Muslims.

So if jihad were a corporate duty, then only some Muslims would be required to participate. However, radicals argue that the verse "fighting is prescribed for you" is an individual duty.

An individual duty does not require permission from any other person to be binding. Therefore Faraj, who wrote his book at the age of twenty-six, took this opportunity to open jihad to young people even if they did not have permission from their parents.

> Let it also be known that if jihad is an individual obligation, then parents' permission is not warranted for going to jihad, as the scholars have said. In this case, it is similar to the individual duties of prayer and fasting.[15]

2. War is for politics, not for preaching faith.

Many people believe that the goal of jihad is to force non-Muslims to accept Islam. Many radicals also think that jihad is for making converts. But Sayyid Qutb insisted that jihad is used to overthrow a government, but preaching—not jihad—is used to make a convert.

Qutb complained that Muslims confused the purpose of jihad with the invitation to accept Islam. They are two separate principles.

The purpose of jihad is to change systems and institutions by force and to bring Muslims and non-Muslims under Islamic law. In contrast, an invitation to accept Islam is voluntary. Qutb wrote:

> This religion forbids the imposition of its belief by force, as is clear from the verse: "There is no compulsion in religion" (Surah 2:256).
>
> Whatever system is to be established in the world ought to be on the authority of God, deriving its laws from Him alone. Then every individual is free, under the protection of this universal system, to adopt any belief he wishes to adopt.[16]

Freedom for Qutb means living under Islamic law but having the ability to choose whether or not to accept the Muslim faith personally. However, if you read the chapter about Islamic law, you understand that living under Islamic law is no kind of freedom.

3. Where to fight

In Islamic thought there is a concept of the "near" enemy and the "far" enemy. The near enemy has been the Muslim governments who are not implementing *sharia* to the satisfaction of the radicals. That is why the early radical groups focused on assassination of people associated with Muslim governments.

As time passed and assassinations were unsuccessful at changing governments, the groups changed their targets, focusing on ways to cause trouble for the government, such as attacking tourists and hurting the tourist industry.

This caused harm to their countries, but it still didn't change the government. Then Al-Qaeda came up with a new strategy: attack the "far" enemy. Al-Qaeda decided that the secular Muslim governments stay in power because of support from the United States. So it began attacks on U.S. interests overseas and then stunned the world by attacking people within the U.S. border on 9/11.

Conclusion

If you were able to meet a suicide bomber on his way to blow up himself or herself, you might say, "You are going to kill yourself and many innocent people. Why? What are you looking for?" They will start their answer with a quote from the Quran:

> O you who believe! Shall I guide you to a trade that will save you from a painful torment? That you believe in Allah and His Messenger (Muhammad), and that you strive hard and fight in the Cause of Allah with your wealth and your lives, that will be better for you, if you but know! (If you do so) He will forgive you your sins, and admit you into Gardens under which rivers flow, and pleasant dwellings in 'Adn (Eden) Paradise; that is indeed the great success. And also (He will give you) another (blessing) which you love,—help from Allah (against your enemies) and a near victory. And give glad tidings (O Muhammad) to the believers.
>
> —Surah 61:10–13

These verses describe a contract between Allah and Muslims. Why is this contract so important? Because of Islamic teaching about paradise.

Through the prophet Muhammad, Allah told mankind to believe in him and follow his law in order to enter paradise. But no matter how hard he tries, every Muslim makes mistakes and commits sin. No direct assurance comes from Allah that his sins will be forgiven. In fact, Islam closes almost every door for Muslims to have that assurance. It doesn't matter how many times they pray or how many good things they do; there is no assurance of forgiveness of sins.

In the midst of that teaching, Islam left a small window open for Muslims to experience assurance of forgiveness. That is the promise from Allah found in this last passage, telling Muslims about the perfect trade. The Muslim must believe in Allah, keep his law, defend Islam, and fight jihad. In response, Allah grants forgiveness of sin and entrance to paradise. The Muslims provide a service for Allah, and Allah pays the price.

On July 7, 2005, four young Muslims blew themselves up on a London bus and on subway trains, killing more than fifty people and injuring more than seven hundred. Do you know why? Because they signed the agreement with Allah.

While the Western media try to figure out all the political and economic reasons for these attacks, the radical Muslims know exactly what is going on. It is a matter of faith. That is why the next and final pillar of radical Islamic philosophy is titled "Faith Is the Reason." Radicals call on Muslims to prove their faith by participating in jihad.

11

PILLAR 5: FAITH IS THE REASON

You will never understand the mind of the Muslim terrorist unless you accept that their foremost motivation is faith. In secular Western society, a discussion of a person's faith is practically considered inappropriate and, in certain circumstances, illegal. But it is ridiculous to try to understand a Muslim radical unless you fully accept that he is acting on the basis of faith.

I run the risk of being accused of oversimplifying the motives of radicals as exclusively based on faith. So I will acknowledge that circumstances in addition to faith can push a person toward radicalism. In other words, if a person is unemployed and suffering under a corrupt government that claims to be Islamic, radicalism will look like the solution to his problems. But these external motives alone will not grip his heart to the point that he would strap on a bomb and blow himself up in the name of the cause. It is the faith factor.

As radical groups are subdued or broken up, it is the faith factor that germinates new groups all across the Islamic world.

If You Believe in Allah, You Will Obey

Dr. Sariah titled his book *The Message of Faith*, and his entire purpose was to explain the foundation of faith that undergirds the radical mind-set. Dr. Sariah said the secret of success of the first Muslims was faith in Allah, as the Quran says, "Therefore fear not men, but fear Me" (Surah 5:44, Ali translation). If you believe, then you will act, wrote Dr. Sariah, even if it means disobeying the president, a minister, an officer, or even a regular policeman on the street. You must obey even if it means jail, loss of job, or worse. If you don't follow the commands of Allah, then you don't believe in Allah. Dr. Sariah wrote:

> If a huge man were attacking you with a gun, and a child was doing the same thing carrying with him a straw of hay, would you be paying any attention to the child?
>
> The answer is of course not; instead, all my attention would be diverted to the man, because if I paid any attention to the child that would mean that I do not believe that the man is actually carrying a gun.... Faith in Allah, must negate any attention to people besides Him, no matter who that person is.[1]

In short, the evidence of faith in Allah is willingness to obey at *any* cost.

If You Believe in Fate, You Will Obey

One of the most important Islamic teachings is about fate. Islam teaches that Allah controls a person's fate—whether a person experiences good or evil, and the hour of death. No amount of human effort can change fate. The Quran says, "No person can ever die except by Allah's Leave and at an appointed term" (Surah 3:145). Therefore, say the radicals, death is nothing to fear because it is under Allah's control.

Dr. Sariah said the first Muslims believed in fate completely, which caused them to be fearless in fighting jihad. "Driven by this ideology, they would act in an unprecedented courage that knows no fear..."[2]

Dr. Sariah also said that if a Muslim fears harm coming to him (jail, job loss, dying) and doesn't follow Allah's command to fight jihad, then he doesn't believe that Allah controls his fate. Not believing in fate makes him an apostate.

If You Believe in Judgment, You Will Obey

Fear of the Last Day, or judgment, is excellent motivation for following Allah's laws, wrote Dr. Sariah, and should be the focus of Islamic teaching.

> Islamic teachings revolve around the idea of fright and appeal (a carrot and a stick), and when we succeed in planting the doctrine of faith in the belief of the Last Day, then we shall succeed in making every individual follow instructions and avoid the prohibited deeds by himself, without the need of us going and wasting our breath in urging the details.[3]

According to Islamic theology, judgment is followed by "eternal fire or eternal bliss." But Dr. Sariah graphically complained that Muslims had evidently lost this belief.

> If...we became truly convinced of these facts about fire and paradise, then it would become impossible for anyone to trot down the road that leads to the fire. So let me illustrate what I am saying: If a man were convicted to spend the rest of his life in a penitentiary, and he knew that inside there will be all kinds of torture, and slashing his flesh with metal knifes, and scorching him with flames all over his sensitive parts, where he had to eat his own flesh, and drink his own urine and other similar methods; then he was offered to leave the penitentiary and be made a king to enjoy all kinds of pleasures of the world, if he did only one thing! Then what would that man choose? Without a doubt he would be ready to sacrifice the whole world, not to become a king, but to save himself the eternal torture. But if that man took an indifferent position to his situation, this means that he does not believe the reality of the prison nor does he believe the verdict of the court.[4]

This description of hell did not come from Dr. Sariah's imagination. He assembled it from the teachings of the Quran and the hadith. Dr. Sariah's point was that if a Muslim believed hell were as bad Allah says it is, then the Muslim would do anything the Quran commands in order to avoid going to hell.

Martyrs Win Paradise

Dr. Sariah went on to reveal that "one thing" that would save a man from "eternal torture"—martyrdom. Martyrdom is reassurance that the ultimate sacrifice receives the ultimate reward.

> There is nothing they could do in life that would guarantee them paradise and salvation from fire, except martyrdom in the cause

> of Allah, and this is evident by the saying of the messenger: "And Allah will not let any one enter the paradise by his work, they said not even you, O messenger of Allah, he said not even me, except that Allah would cover me with His mercy."[5]

Islam teaches that on Judgment Day a man's deeds are weighed, and then Allah decides if he may enter paradise. If you live as an infidel, you may be sure of going to hell. But if you live the best Muslim life you possibly can, you still have no guarantee of entering paradise, as the quote from the Quran explained. There is only one guarantee—martyrdom.

The teaching that martyrs will go to paradise is so widely accepted in Islam that the radicals don't even take the time to quote justification from the Quran and hadith. However, the Western reader would benefit from seeing this information, so I will provide one quote each from the Quran and the hadith.

The Quran says:

> Think not of those who are killed in the Way of Allah as dead. Nay, they are alive, with their Lord, and they have provision. They rejoice in what Allah has bestowed upon them of His Bounty, rejoicing for the sake of those who have not yet joined them, but are left behind (not yet martyred) that on them no fear shall come, nor shall they grieve. They rejoice in a Grace and a Bounty from Allah, and that Allah will not waste the reward of the believers.
>
> —Surah 3:169–171

These verses were written specifically about participation in jihad, not about dying of other causes. In hadith, Muhammad clearly promised that a martyr's reward is paradise.

> The Prophet said, "The person who participates in (Holy battles) in Allah's cause and nothing compels him to do so except belief in Allah and His Apostles, will be recompensed by Allah either with a reward, or booty (if he survives) or will be admitted to Paradise (if he is killed in the battle as a martyr)."[6]

If you have no other motive for participating in jihad, says Dr. Sariah, at least remember the coveted gift of martyrdom.

> Martyrdom is the subject of enumerable verses and speeches, and if a Muslim becomes convinced of that, it becomes the most coveted desire that he seeks, even the only hope in life, as it is the only guaranteed way which rescues him from the fire and ushers him to the highest levels of paradise.[7]

Death Is Not Defeat

Death is not defeat for the Islamic radical.

Qutb prepared his followers for opposition and fortified them with the concept that they would triumph because they are believers. "So do not become weak (against your enemy), nor be sad, and you will be superior (in victory) if you are indeed (true) believers" (Surah 3:139).

However, this triumph may or may not be in this world. Sayyid Qutb, in his scholarly way, turned the death of a Muslim fighter into an act of nobility, as he wrote:

> Conditions change, the Muslim loses his physical power and is conquered: yet the consciousness does not depart from him that he is the most superior. If he remains a Believer, he looks upon his conqueror from a superior position.... Even if death is his portion, he will never bow his head. Death comes to all, but for him there is martyrdom. He will proceed to the Garden, while his conquerors go to the Fire.[8]

Although martyrdom is a great honor, Qutb wanted his followers to know that the greatest of rewards was "the pleasure of Allah."[9]

Superiority of Islam and Its Followers

A repeated theme in Islamic teaching is that the believer is superior—superior in faith, in his understanding and concept of the nature of the world, in his values and standards, in conscience and understanding, and in law and life. "He is the most superior and the rest are all in an inferior position. From his height he looks at them with dignity and honour, and with compassion and sympathy for their condition, and with a desire to guide them to the good which he has and to lift them up to the horizon where he lives."[10]

A religious radical believes secular society is hostile to him, but he ultimately expects to pay back their insults. Qutb wrote:

> The Believer holds on to his religion like the holder of a precious stone in the society devoid of religion, of character, or high values, of noble manners and of whatever is clean, pure and beautiful. The others mock his tenacity, ridicule his ideas, laugh at his values, but this does not make the Believer weak of heart; and he looks from his height at those who mock, ridicule and laugh, and he says, as one of the great souls—those who preceded him on the long and bright path of faith,—Noah, said: "You ridicule us! Yet indeed we shall ridicule you as you ridicule" (Surah 11:38).[11]

Fighting for the Faith

It is human nature to transfer your own opinions onto other people. In that vein, the radicals see their enemies as motivated by religion because they themselves are motivated by religion. For example, in its 1998 fatwa, Al-Qaeda said that the American aims behind the first Gulf War were first "religious" and then "economic."

The idea that unbelievers attack the Muslim for his faith is powerful and dangerous. Muslim radicals are highly motivated if they view the enemy as trying to wipe out Islam. This mind-set is rooted in a well-known Quranic story called the Makers of the Pit.

The Makers of the Pit

In the Makers of the Pit (Surah 85:1–16), a group of believers encountered a group of unbelievers who tortured them to try to make them give up their faith. The believers were burned alive as their tormentors laughed. The Quran said:

> They had no fault except that they believed in Allah, the All-Mighty, Worthy of all Praise!
>
> —Surah 85:8

In the same way, Sayyid Qutb said society had turned against the radicals because of their faith.

> This was a question of belief and a battle of belief. The Believers ought to be certain of this.... They are their enemies only because of their belief.... The enemies of the Believers may wish to change this struggle into an economic or political or racial struggle, so that the Believers become confused concerning the true nature of the struggle and the flame of belief in their hearts

> become extinguished. The Believers must not be deceived and must understand that this is a trick.[12]

In short, economic, political, and racial motives are inferior to the Muslim's most important goal—defending and restoring Islam.

Conclusion

I am always surprised—and disappointed—at how difficult it is for Western media to acknowledge that "faith is the reason" behind radical Islamic groups. However, one segment of Western society does have a natural understanding of the mind-set of a Muslim fundamentalist, and that is the Christian fundamentalist. As a Christian myself, I don't say this in a derogatory manner. I simply mean that Christians can identify with the Muslim's "faith factor."

Qutb is a classic fundamentalist who is convinced that Islam is the perfect foundation for life. For example, Qutb declared that the Quran "discusses all minor or major affairs of mankind; it orders man's life—not only of this world but also of the world to come."[13] Every fundamental Christian would say the same of the Bible.

In addition, Qutb complained that "society is devoid of those vital values which are necessary not only for its healthy development but also for its real progress."[14] However, diagnosing a problem is not the same as having the correct solution. In fact, this points to part of the appeal of the radical movement: its leaders diagnose problems in Muslim society that its people recognize as real, but the radicals offer a horrible solution to these problems.

So, both Christian and Muslim fundamentalists call for a restoration of morality and a return to Scripture. What is the difference between the two? The difference is in their Scriptures. Fundamentalist Christians are not forming terrorist cells and bombing civilians because Jesus did not set this kind of example. The Quran calls for a completely different lifestyle than the Bible. In short, the essential difference between Muslim and Christian fundamentalists is their founders.

Section 5 of this book takes you to the place where the terrorists found their Five Pillars of Radical Philosophy—the lives of Muhammad and his followers. But before I present that information, I want to offer one more warning about radicals. Every person involved in the war on terror needs to know that radicals consider deceit to be one of their most important strategies. The next section will tell how radicals apply Islamic teaching about deceit to their daily lives.

SECTION 4
WARNING ABOUT DECEIT

12

DECEPTION: AN ART OF WAR PRACTICED BY RADICALS

In the Muslim world, Muhammad is well known for declaring, "War is deceit."[1] In other words, Islam teaches that deception is one of the essential tools of jihad. In the next two chapters my purpose is to warn the world about why and how radicals will use deceit.

Chapter thirteen will show you:

- The hadith that gives Muslims permission to lie during war

- Islamic law about Muslims lying when they are living in a non-Muslim country

- The Shiite tradition of lying to conceal true feelings (*at-toqya*)

- Muhammad's use of deceit in assassinating his enemies

Chapter fourteen is very unique because it is my translation of al-Zawahiri's teaching about deceit that I found posted in Arabic on a radical Web site. These teachings are very important because they are not just talk. They are being put in action every day by Al-Qaeda and other radicals. In this book, which is titled *Covert Operations*, al-Zawahiri goes deep into Islamic history to find new strategies of deceit that he can use in the fight against infidels.

An ordinary, secular Muslim may not be aware of these teachings, but I assure you that any imam trained in the Middle East knows about them, and you need to know about them, too.

THREE TIMES TO LIE

Lying was a widespread practice among Muslims until Muhammad realized that it was turning into a grave danger threatening the growth of his message in Arabia. This caused him to rebuke his followers one day, declaring, "Why do I see you flocking into lying, as butterflies flock into the fire? All lying will be written against the sons of Adam except if he lies in war, or when two men are quarreling and he mediates between them, or fabricates (lies) to his wife to please her."[2]

In other words, Muhammad objected to lying in some matters, but he approved Muslims lying under three circumstances:

1. During war
2. To reconcile between two feuding parties
3. To a spouse in order to please her

Even though the social circumstances for lying are very interesting, we will focus our attention on lying "during war."

LYING IN THE HOUSE OF WAR

Deceit during war takes different forms and different shapes. If Muslims shows acceptance, friendliness, and sociability toward their enemy, the enemy should not be lulled into thinking they are completely safe and sound from them. For example, radical groups have often used peace treaties to give them time to resupply and prepare to continue to fight in the future.

It's important to understand that radical groups use deceit in different ways, depending on what phase of jihad they are in. Radicals divide jihad into three phases.

PHASE 1 OF JIHAD: POWERLESSNESS

In this phase Muslims are a minority living in a non-Muslim country; therefore, they are not required to fight against the enemies. Rather, they are required to be patient as they wait to enter the second phase. Deceit may become part of daily life for a Muslim in this position. They are practicing Muhammad's words: "All lying is a sin except the one benefiting the Muslim or the one keeping him out of harm's way."

The Sheikh of Islam, Ibn Taymiyyah, applied Muhammad's teaching this way:

> If a believer [Muslim] is in a land where he is the weaker, or at a time when he is the weaker, let him then go by the virtue of patience, forgiving and pardoning those of the Jews and the Christians who hurt Allah and his Messenger, and he shall lie to them, if that was a way of preserving his life and his religion.[3]

On what did Ibn Taymiyyah base this philosophy? It came from the life of Muhammad. Let's look at the first incident in which the prophet of Islam authorized Muslims to lie and deny their faith in order to protect themselves.

A slave named Ammar Bin Yasser had become a Muslim, and he was being tortured by the tribe of Quraysh. They demanded that he forfeit his faith in order for them to stop the torture, so he denied his faith. After they let him go, he hurried to Muhammad and told him what had happened.

Muhammad asked him, "Was anything of that from the heart?" (Meaning, "Was there any change in your faith?")

Yasser answered no.

Muhammad replied, "If they come again, do it again (meaning if they catch you and torture you again, go ahead and lie to them again)."[4]

In other words, if a Muslim is in a weak position, he may deny his faith in order to stop persecution from an enemy. A modern orthodox Islamic theologian (Al Mansour) said succinctly:

> If you are incapable of cutting the hand of your enemy, then kiss it.[5]

In other words, if you have to pretend to be submissive in order to deceive your enemy, then do so even if in your heart you are not. Muhammad "kissed many hands" during his time in Mecca simply because he could not "cut them off."

Shielding

The Shiite sect of Islam has a special term for lying when a person is in a position of powerlessness. They call it *shielding* (*at-toqya* in Arabic), meaning, "cloaking, obscuring, or concealing." The shielding philosophy developed because the Shiites were severely persecuted by the Sunnis during the Umayyad Dynasty. For Shiites, shielding means that a Muslim thinks or believes one thing but reveals another. An example is when one holds hatred toward someone but displays love and forgiveness toward him.

The Shiites showed nothing but love to the Umayyads, while keeping detestation and anger in their hearts. The followers of Ali preserved this custom and applied it in their beliefs for more than thirteen hundred years.

The only time Shiites abandoned shielding was after Ayatollah Khomeini successfully led the revolution against the shah of Iran in 1979. Right after Khomeini arrived in Tehran from Paris, he read a short speech at the Paradise Graveyard and declared to the whole world and to the Shiites that the time of shielding was over. By that he meant that the Shiites were in charge and they could reveal their true feelings because they were now the ones in power.[6]

PHASE 2 OF JIHAD: PREPARATION

In this phase, the Muslims are required to gather their resources in order to enter a direct and real war against their enemies. During the first year after his immigration to Medina, Muhammad and his army were in the preparation phase.

PHASE 3 OF JIHAD: ENTERING INTO WAR WITH NON-MUSLIMS

In this phase, Muslims convert from sitting patiently into actively moving toward altering the conditions around them and changing the country into a new Islamic country.

After Muhammad became sure of his power in Medina, he entered the third phase where he engaged in direct confrontations with his enemies. He killed the men, took the women and the children captive, and distributed the captives as spoils of war among his men. These captives eventually became slaves that were bought and sold in the markets, which gained a remarkable fame in the Arabian Peninsula. He tracked down his enemies one by one until he was capable of returning to Mecca and defeating its armies.

Lying is completely authorized to the Muslim during war, and it is a vital factor of victory. Muhammad's phrase "war is deception"

(*Al-harb khida'a*) is widely known and quoted. Deceit is an acknowledged part of strategy, as Faraj wrote:

> The scholars of Islam have agreed to the legitimacy of deceiving the idolaters during war by any means unless it was preceded by an agreement or a treaty; then it is not allowed. And it is known that there is no treaty or agreement between us [Al-Jihad] and them [Egyptian government], as they are combatants to the religion of Allah. The Muslims are then free to choose any appropriate method of fighting they deem fit, as long as the trick accomplishes victory with the least amount of losses.[7]

Faraj recounted three gruesome stories from Islamic history as examples of good use of deceit. Most westerners would be shocked at the type of behavior that is lauded as heroic and worthy of emulation. I will summarize these stories for you.

THE BEHEADING OF THE REBELLIOUS POET

Muhammad asked a group of his friends, "Who will take care of Kaab bin Ashraf [a poet who was criticizing Muhammad] for me?"

A man named Muhammad bin Musslemah said, "Would you like me to kill him?"

Muhammad responded, "Yes."

Musslemah answered, "Permit me to say things [meaning to lie]."

Muhammad gave him permission.

Musslemah went to the poet and pretended to be displeased with Muhammad and in need of a loan. He convinced the poet to allow him to secure the loan with weapons and promised to return the following night.

So Musslemah came back the next night with two men [and the weapons] and went out for a walk with the poet. As the poet and Musslemah walked, Musslemah held him by the hair as if to kiss [greet] him and held him while the other two men ambushed him and cut off his head.

Muhammad justified the assassination by saying: "If he [the poet] had stayed silent just as everyone who shared his same opinion stayed, he wouldn't have been murdered. But he harmed us with his poetry, and any one of you who did that would have deserved the sword."

Praising the cleverness of this incident, Faraj commented, "In this story, there are many useful lessons in the art of war."

The beheading of a rebel leader

Muhammad heard of a man named Abi Sufyan who was trying to gather an army to go to war against Muhammad. So Muhammad ordered a man named Abdullah to kill him. Abdullah asked permission to lie, which Muhammad granted. So Abdullah went to Abi Sufyan and pretended to be interested in joining the uprising. He complained about Muhammad and won Abi Sufyan's trust enough to join him in his tent that night. After everyone else fell asleep, Abdullah cut off the man's head and then took it to Muhammad.

The spy who pretended not to have converted

A man from an enemy tribe converted to Islam, but Muhammad told him to return to his tribe and pretend not to have converted. The man went back and spread false information among his people about the battle they were about to fight with Muhammad.

Obligation to Deceive

Muslim radicals of today look at deceit as an art of war that was used by the prophet himself. They study the different incidents of deception in Muhammad's life to develop a modern picture of the principle of deception, particularly during the preparation phase of jihad. They use deception in communication to recruit new members. They use it in buying weapons. They use it in negotiation or cease-fire.

Because the prophet of Islam established this principle, Muslim radicals see deceit as something sacred that they not only have the right to do but are obligated to do. They look at deception as a way to save the life of Muslims and achieve victory over the enemy. This is exactly the position of Ayman al-Zawahiri, second in command of Al-Qaeda. That's why he wrote an entire book about how jihad fighters should use deception. In this next chapter you can read about the specific strategies he recommends.

13

AL-ZAWAHIRI'S TEACHINGS ON DECEIT

Ayman al-Zawahiri leads a busy terrorist organization, and he must solve practical problems. For example, he may want some Al-Qaeda members to blend in and live in the United States. If these men wore full beards and went to ultraconservative mosques to pray, then they would arouse suspicion and get put on a watch list. Instead, al-Zawahiri would want these operatives to go undercover and blend into society. However, these devout Muslims will not go undercover unless they believe they have permission to do so from the teachings of Islam.

As a result, al-Zawahiri wrote a booklet titled *Covert Operations,* which goes deep into Islamic teaching and history to describe how deceit can be a tool in a Muslim's life.*

LYING IN WAR AND IN PEACE

In the beginning of the book, al-Zawahiri cited the hadith that gives Muslims permission to lie in three circumstances, including during war (as you learned in the previous chapter). But al-Zawahiri went into more detail about using deceit during peace if it will "protect the believers from harm from the infidels." He said the greatest example of this was Abraham.[1]

First, Abraham claimed that his wife, Sara, was actually his sister because he was afraid the king would kill him to take her. (See Surah 37 and compare to Genesis 20.) Second, Abraham lied by saying, "I am

* The entire book by al-Zawahiri is posted at the Arabic language Web site for al-Tawheed wal-Jihad (The Pulpit of Monotheism and Jihad), which is the radical group headed by al-Zaraqawi in Iraq and affiliated with Al-Qaeda: www.tawhed.ws/r?i=2638

sick" so that his family would leave him alone in the temple of idols so he could destroy the idols. (See Surah 37:89 and compare to the story of Gideon in Judges 6.) According to the Islamic teaching, Abraham's use of deceit was a good thing.

Hiding Faith

Hiding faith in order to live undercover is a major stumbling block for Muslims because they grow up hearing that Islam must be practiced and spread openly. The Quran says:

> O Messenger (Muhammad)! Proclaim (the Message) which has been sent down to you from your Lord. And if you do not, then you have not conveyed His Message.
>
> —Surah 5:67

> Therefore proclaim openly (Allah's Message—Islamic Monotheism) that which you are commanded.
>
> —Surah 15:94; see also Surah 4:165

Al-Zawahiri acknowledged "Islam is obviously a public religion. You do things publicly, not in secret." Yet Zawahiri pointed out that the first years of Islam were totally different. Muhammad hid his call and told only the people closest to him until Allah gave him permission to speak.

Muhammad told one new believer: "O Abizar, keep it secret and go back to your place and when you hear that we declared Islam publicly, come back to us."[2]

In the first years, some Muslims prayed in secret: "Hudhaifa reported...We actually suffered trial so much so that some of our men were constrained to offer their prayers in concealment."[3]

The Quran also spoke of a "believing man of Fir'aun's (Pharaoh's) family, who hid his faith" (Surah 40:28; see also Surah 18:19).

Therefore, al-Zawahiri concluded that "hiding one's faith and being secretive was allowed especially in time of fear from persecution of the infidels."

This logic gives Muslims permission to blend into society if it will keep them safe and further their goals. By living like typical Americans, they avoid suspicion from authorities who are taught that a radical Muslim would not live that way.

Al-Zawahiri specifically gave radicals permission not to pray in the mosque or attend Friday sermons if it would compromise their position. He quoted from the famous legal scholar Ibn Hanbali:

> Muslims are allowed not to pray in the mosque or attend Friday prayer if they fear the enemy. And the justification came through the word of the prophet Muhammad, who said Muslims are allowed to do that if they have fear or sickness. And the fear is divided into three categories: fear for himself, fear for his money, and fear for his family. The first category includes fear from the government, an enemy, thieves or a dangerous animal.[4]

Al-Zawahiri sealed his argument with a very important quote from Ibn Taymiyyah (which I also mentioned in chapter twelve). Read these words carefully and remember that the radical is going to follow them literally:

> If someone from the believers is in a land or a time of persecution, he has to use the verse of patience and forgiveness about people of the book (Christians or hte Jews) and *el Mushrikun* (idol worshippers) who are doing harm to Allah and his apostle.

Al-Zawahiri told believers to practice patience and forgiveness when they are weak. But when they have power, he told them to follow Surah 9:5, which says:

> Kill the *Mushrikun* (see V.2:105) wherever you find them, and capture them and besiege them, and prepare for them each and every ambush.

Deceit in Battle

Al-Zawahiri reminded his readers of two specific ways Muhammad used deceit in battle.

1. Keeping battle plans secret.

> Whenever Allah's Apostle intended to carry out a Ghazwa (battle), he would use an equivocation to conceal his real destination until the Ghazwa of Tabuk which Allah's Apostle carried out in very hot weather. As he was going to face a very long journey

> through a wasteland and was to meet and attack a large number of enemies. So he made the situation clear to the Muslims so that they might prepare themselves accordingly and get ready to conquer their enemy.[5]

This hadith describes a lot of battle strategy. First it says that Muhammad normally did not reveal where he was taking his troops to fight. But he made an exception for the battle of Tabuk because it was a long, hot journey, and he wanted to allow the troops to prepare.

2. Spying

Muhammad frequently sent spies to discover the preparation and plans of the enemies. For example:

> Allah's Apostle sent a Sariya of ten men as spies under the leadership of 'Asim bin Thabit al-Ansari, the grandfather of 'Asim bin Umar Al-Khattab.[6]

The hadith also mention that Muhammad ordered the death of several people who were suspected of spying on him.

> "An infidel spy came to the Prophet while he was on a journey. The spy sat with the companions of the Prophet and started talking and then went away. The Prophet said (to his companions), 'Chase and kill him.' So, I killed him." The Prophet then gave him the belongings of the killed spy (in addition to his share of the war booty).[7]

Conclusion

Remember, al-Zawahiri is not dead or in prison. He is active and teaching radicals to use these strategies. The book is on the Web site for anyone in the world with a computer and the ability to understand Arabic to read. This should make us all uncomfortable.

The next section of this book takes you to the place where the terrorists found their Five Pillars of Radical Philosophy—the lives of Muhammad and his followers.

SECTION 5
FOLLOWING MUHAMMAD'S FOOTSTEPS

14

MUHAMMAD: UNCENSORED

A Muslim radical is a fundamentalist: he wants to follow the example of Muhammad and his companions as closely as possible. He wants to bring the seventh century to life again in the twenty-first century. So to understand the radical mind-set, you must know the story of his prophet.

Perhaps you have already learned about the life of Muhammad. If so, you may be tempted to skip this chapter, and if you choose to do so, that is fine. However, let me mention that you may not have heard the story the way that I am going to tell it to you now. It is the uncensored version.

By "uncensored version" I mean that there is a tendency on the part of westerners who write about Islam to filter out the parts that would be distasteful to their Western audience. The Muslim radicals do not appreciate this gesture. Instead, they usually think the westerners are maliciously trying to convey an inaccurate picture of their beliefs.[1]

So this account is not westernized. It is simply the story the way that Islamic history records it.

Gabriel Visits

The story begins in Mecca, Saudi Arabia, with the birth of Muhammad on August 2, A.D. 570. With Muhammad's birth came the birth of Islam, though not publicly announced until he was in his forties. In the year 610, Muhammad went to a cave in the mountains surrounding Mecca to meditate, and he came back declaring that the manifestation of the archangel Gabriel came to him and gave him the first verse of the Quran:

> By the Qur'an, full of Wisdom,—you are indeed one of the Messengers, on a Straight Way. It is a Revelation sent down by (Him), the Exalted in Might, Most Merciful, in order that thou mayest admonish a people, whose fathers had received no admonition, and who therefore remain heedless (of the Signs of Allah).
>
> —Surah 36:2–6, Ali translation

Cooperation and Tolerance

With this divine endorsement, Muhammad preached in Mecca for about thirteen years, offering his ideas and his message to its people and its visitors, especially those who would come as pilgrims from all over the Arabian Peninsula to the idol shrine in Mecca.

Muhammad had great ambitions, but despite his efforts, only a handful of people believed during those first thirteen years. New converts were persecuted and the leading tribe led a boycott against the Muslims and Muhammad's clan for several years. His great opportunity came when he was asked to mediate an ancient conflict between two major tribes in Medina, a city not too far from Mecca. His success resulted in these two tribes accepting Islam and making a pact to defend and protect him.

Power and Growth

Overnight Muhammad went from a persecuted leader of a handful of people to an affluent tribal lord with thousands of followers. No longer was he forced to tolerate the harassment and disdain of his tribe, the Quraysh. Muhammad, now fifty-three years old, left Mecca and joined his new followers in Medina, starting a new page in the story of Islam. This is a very significant event in the minds of Muslim radicals. It marks the end of restrained, subservient Islam and the beginning of Islam with power. Known as *hijra,* Muhammad's move marks the beginning of the Islamic calendar.

The new, aggressive stance of Islam began with the Battle of Badr, which Muhammad initiated against the tribes of his hometown of Mecca—and won. During the next six years, Muhammad's military forced the Arabs to recognize Muhammad's political program.

Muhammad assured his followers that he was not going to fight his enemies by power alone but that Allah and his angels were going to carry the swords and fight with them against anyone who stood against Muhammad or refused to accept Islam.[2]

With Allah by their side, Muhammad and his army set their sights on conquering the world. This is the Muhammad that the Islamic radical is emulating. Muhammad personally led his army into twenty-six battles, and they were very successful. The motley group that began in a desolate city in the desert subdued the cities of Arabia one by one until, right before his death, Muhammad had total control of the entire Arabian Peninsula.

His religious, political, and military empire threatened all the neighboring countries and kingdoms. Through his teachings and decisions regarding disputes, Muhammad taught Muslims how to deal with each other and how to deal with their enemies. He drew a complete picture of the philosophy of war, describing in detail methods of attack and retreat, fighting and killing, who would be killed, who would be spared, prisoners, and spoils of war.

The Book of Jihad

If you put one of today's radicals on trial and asked him how he defined jihad, he would say, "Look at the Book of Jihad in *al-Bukhari*. That is how I define jihad." What does this mean? Islamic scholar al-Bukhari (A.H. 194–256) compiled the most respected collection of stories about Muhammad's teachings and actions. He loosely organized the stories into books according to topic, and book 52 is titled, "Fighting for the Cause of Allah (Jihad)." So the terrorist on trial would say, "Muhammad's way of jihad is my way of jihad."

Book 52 of al-Bukhari is no secret. You can go to the University of Southern California Web site and read it for yourself in English any time you want. (Go to http://www.usc.edu/dept/MSA/. Go to "tools" and click on "hadith.") You will find that the Book of Jihad contains about two hundred stories from the life of Muhammad that:

- Extol the virtue of jihad (as a physical fight).
- Promise reward for jihad.
- Give accounts of particular battles.
- Describe the value of horses for jihad.
- Give rules about prayer during jihad.

The Book of Jihad promises the radical that the reward for fighting jihad is greater than any other reward.

> A man came to Allah's Apostle and said, "Instruct me as to such a deed as equals Jihad (in reward)." He replied, "I do not find such a deed." Then he added, "Can you, while the Muslim fighter is in the battle-field, enter your mosque to perform prayers without ceasing and fast and never break your fast?" The man said, "But who can do that?" Abu-Huraira added, "The Mujahid (i.e. Muslim fighter) is rewarded even for the footsteps of his horse while it wanders about (for grazing) tied in a long rope."[3]

Can you imagine how the radical is reassured by these words? As long as he is engaged in jihad, even during those times when the horse is grazing (metaphorically speaking), the radical is reassured that he is earning his reward.

Radicals also rally around the following quote from Muhammad:

> Allah's Apostle said, "Know that Paradise is under the shades of swords."[4]

I wish, however, that all radicals would honor the following hadith:

> During some of the Ghazawat of Allah's Apostle a woman was found killed, so Allah's Apostle *forbade* the killing of women and children.[5]

Muhammad did not agree with targeting women and children, so when radicals attack a group of Muslim children who are getting candy from American soldiers, the radicals should be condemned by their own peers. The same goes for the murder of Russian schoolchildren by the Chechnyens. Muhammad would condemn them.

POLITICS AND RELIGION GO TOGETHER

Muhammad completely fused together religion and politics in the Islamic world. He was the prophet and the messenger, but at the same time he was the political leader. Islamic history records the details of his system. He had thirty-six princes in his government, and his two closest friends, Abu Bakr and Umar ibn Al-Khattib, were his aides. He appointed four judges as well as a finance minister and three counselors.

Twenty-five scribes were assigned to copy the Quran as well as Muhammad's messages to other leaders. Seven men were in charge of law enforcement.

Muhammad appointed two men to handle matters related to his dwelling and running the affairs of his house—Ali ibn Abu Talib and Bilal bin Rabah. Thirteen of Muhammad's friends were specially designated to carry his flags when going to raids or battles.

Idealized Picture of Early Islam

The eleven years that Muhammad ruled from Medina represent to the Islamic radicals the ideal society that they are striving to achieve. No one describes this society more gloriously than the founder of modern Islamic terrorism, Sayyid Qutb:

> The society was freed from all oppression, and the Islamic system was established in which justice was God's justice and in which weighing was by God's balance....
>
> Morals were elevated, hearts and souls were purified, and with the exception of a very few cases, there was no occasion even to enforce the limits and punishments which God has prescribed; for now conscience was the law-enforcer and the pleasure of Allah, the hope of Divine reward, and the fear of Allah's anger took the place of police and punishments.
>
> Mankind was uplifted in its social order, in its morals in all of its life, to a zenith of perfection which had never been attained before and which cannot be attained afterwards except through Islam.[6]

What a beautiful picture he paints! For those who know little about Islamic history, the appeal of this description is powerful. From my perspective, however, and with my doctorate degree in Islamic culture and history from Al-Azhar University, this picture is a fantasy.

Let's look at some of the events that occurred in this perfect society. Some are recorded in the Quran, and others are a part of the hadith. I encourage you to look up these stories for yourself.

Enforcing the law

Qutb said that except for a very few cases, there was no occasion to enforce Islamic law. Here are a few of those exceptions: A woman was convicted of adultery, and she was pregnant. Muhammad commanded that she be allowed to give birth to the child. After the child was weaned, Muhammad took the child from the woman, gave it to another family, and ordered the woman to be buried up to her neck and stoned to death.[7]

Another woman was caught stealing and brought before the prophet by some who wanted her sentence to be softened. Muhammad said, "No, even if it were my own daughter caught stealing, the sentence is the same." So they cut off her hand in accordance with Islamic law.[8] Before this time, Arabian society had never punished stealing by cutting off a hand.

Perfection of morality

Qutb also said that morals had reached a "zenith of perfection." Consider these examples:

Muhammad was angry with a poet who was criticizing him, so he gathered his followers and asked who would take care of this poet. One volunteered, but he told Muhammad that he would have to lie in order to kill him. Muhammad said, "Do it."[9]

Muhammad conquered a Jewish village and needed to decide what to do with the captives. One of his advisors said, "You should kill all the men." Muhammad agreed, and the Muslim army killed all the Jewish men as their wives and children watched. Muhammad was attracted to one of the wives whose husband he had just killed, so he took her and married her.[10]

The bottom line is that Islamic radicals present an unrealistic (or incomplete) picture of the glories of the first Islamic community as part of their recruiting strategy. Therefore, young people who do not have a complete understanding of Islamic history are more vulnerable. On the other hand, those who are learning Islamic history through a school such as Al-Azhar resist the recruiters because they can see the selective way that the radicals are using history.

There are some aspects of Muhammad's life, however, to which the Islamic radicals are completely faithful. Muhammad's final sermon to his followers provides an excellent example.

Muhammad's Last Days

At a gathering of one hundred thousand Muslims in Mecca for the first *hajj*, Muhammad stood on Mount Arafat and delivered what would be his farewell sermon to Arabia and the whole world. He concluded, "After today there will no longer be two religions existing in Arabia. I descended by Allah with the sword in my hand, and my wealth will come from the shadow of my sword. And the one who will disagree with me will be humiliated and persecuted."[11]

Please make note of the phrase: "There will no longer be two religions existing in Arabia." This comment is one of the key reasons behind radical Muslims being offended at the presence of any non-Muslims on the Arabian Peninsula.

Muhammad also says that Allah sent him "with the sword." In other words, the sword has divine approval, and Muhammad made no apology for using it to bring wealth to the Muslims. He also promised that this sword would humiliate and persecute those who disagree with him. Again, this is the Muhammad the Islamic radicals emulate.

Incidentally, moderate Muslims also know these stories about Muhammad. That is why they can be slow to condemn the actions of the radicals. Deep inside, they wonder if perhaps the radicals are doing the best job of following Muhammad's example after all.

After this famous sermon, Muhammad developed a fever, which lasted twenty days and ended in his death at the age of sixty-four.

The Next Stage

I can only describe the next 650 years after Muhammad's death as a bloodbath, from beginning to end. To say otherwise would be to distort history.

Why is Islamic history so violent? First, it had violent beginnings as Muhammad led raids against non-Muslims around him. Second, Muslims were deeply committed to following Muhammad's example.

In the next chapter you will get to see how the leaders of Islam after Muhammad were faithful to his legacy.

THE FOUR MAJOR CALIPHATES OF ISLAMIC HISTORY

Islamic history can get very detailed and confusing, but it doesn't have to be that way. To help you get an overall picture, here is a simple overview of the four major caliphates that led the Muslim world up to the twentieth century.*

A.H. 11–40 (A.D. 632–661)	The Four Rightly Guided Caliphs Abu Bakr Umar ibn Al-Khattib Uthman bin Affan Ali ibn Abu Talib	29 years
A.H. 41–132 (A.D. 661–751)	Umayyad Dynasty	90 years
A.H. 132–656 (A.D. 750–1258)	Abbasid State (defeated by Mongols in A.H. 656/A.D. 1258)	508 years
(A.D. 1301–1924)	Ottoman Empire (dismantled by Kamil Attaturk in 1924)	623 years

* Let me also give you a little explanation about the difference between A.H. and A.D. dating. The Islamic calendar marks dates according to A.H. or after *hijra*. Therefore a date such as A.H. 5 refers to the fifth year after Muhammad immigrated to Medina. For understanding Islamic history, it is helpful to see A.H. dates because they show you the year in relationship to when Muhammad lived. Keep in mind, however, that the Islamic calendar is based on a lunar month, which means that an A.H. year is not exactly the same length as an A.D. year. This makes it difficult to make an exact collaboration between A.H. and A.D. dates unless you know the month and day as well. In the chart below, the length of the caliphates are noted in A.D. years.

15

THE UNRELENTING BLOODBATH

After Muhammad died, the Muslim community was temporarily divided on choosing a caliph (successor), but they finally decided upon Abu Bakr, sixty years old, who was Muhammad's first male convert and the father of Muhammad's favorite wife, Aisha.

The Rightly Guided Caliphs (A.H. 11–40/A.D. 632–661)

Abu Bakr and the three leaders who followed him became known as the "rightly guided" caliphs because they tried to enforce Islam and protect Islamic society in the same way Muhammad did. However, in the space of only twenty-nine years, we can observe:

- The first caliph killing eighty thousand Muslims for not paying taxes
- The second caliph aggressively attacking the nations bordering Arabia in order to expand the empire
- The third caliph being assassinated by Muslim rebels (the Kharij) because he was showing favoritism to his family
- The fourth caliph fighting a rebellion from the governor of Syria for not avenging the murder of the third caliph

Rather than studying each caliph in detail, we will look at the two events from this period that have had the most impact on radical philosophy.

Event #1: Crushing the first rebellion

Immediately after the first caliph, Abu Bakr, took control, he faced a rebellion: many of the new Muslim converts refused to pay the tax (*zakat*), which is one of the five pillars of Islam. Abu Bakr chose to dramatically enforce his authority, and he sent his famous general, Khalid ibn Walid, known as "the Sword of Allah," to subdue them. It was a bitter, bloody conflict, and in only three months, Khalid killed eighty thousand of the rebellious Muslims.

At one point Abu Bakr was asked why he had chosen to take such a hard-line stance against those who refused to pay the tax since they had agreed to all the other tenets of Islam.

> ... Omar ibn Al-Khattab asked Abu Bakr, "Why do you fight these people, when the prophet has said 'I was ordered to fight these people until they would utter the words "No god except Allah," then after that they would have protected themselves and their belongings from me, except what he would still owe to Allah on his accord.'"
>
> Abu Bakr then said, "By Allah if they had denied me a head dress that they would be normally giving to the messenger I would fight them for it."
>
> So Omar said, "By Allah, then I saw that the Almighty Allah had prepared Abu Bakr's heart for war, and I knew then that it was righteousness."[1]

This immediate policy of submission through force would be the norm for the next six and a half centuries of Islam.

Event #2: Islam torn into two parts

The rule of the fourth caliph revealed a trend that remains imbedded in the Muslim community to this day: Muslims using Islamic law to fight against each other.

The governor of Syria, Muawiyya, argued that Islamic law required the fourth caliph, Ali ibn Abu Talib, to punish those who killed the third caliph (a rebel group called the Kharijites). However, Ali refused because he feared that a punishment would cause the insurrection to spread. So Muawiyya said Ali had defied Islamic law and was no longer the legitimate ruler.

Ali, on the other hand, said that as the caliph, he represented the prophet Muhammad, and Muhammad would never tolerate his followers to rebel against him. Ali called Muawiyya's rebellion a monumental desecration of the Islamic law and common law that had been followed since Muhammad's time.

With both sides using Islamic law and Muhammad's example to support their claims, this conflict caused the Muslims to be divided into two camps—the Sunni led by Muawiyya and the Shiite led by Ali. They fought many battles, but in the end Ali was killed and Muawiyya took control of the empire, beginning the Umayyad Dynasty (A.H. 41–132/A.D. 661–751).

Umayyad Dynasty (A.H. 41–132/A.D. 661–751)

I have a special affinity with the Umayyad Dynasty, so to speak, because it was the focus of my master's thesis at Al-Azhar University in Cairo, Egypt. The ruthlessness and treachery of infighting for power in the Islamic empire at this time amazed me.

The Kharijites (who had assassinated the third caliph) continued to rebel against the caliphate, diverting the Islamic army from its primary duty of conquest because it had to stay within the empire to control them.

Muawiyya used any available method to rid himself of his enemies—by assassination, or poisoning, or even collective annihilation, which is how he ended the Kharij movement.

Muawiyya passed the throne to his son Yazid, who defeated another rebel group led by Al-Hussein ibn Ali, who was Muhammad's grandson (the son of Muhammad's daughter Fatima). Instead of sparing Al-Hussein's life out of respect for Muhammad, Yazid killed his family, beheaded him, and carried the head back to the palace in Damascus to put on display.

The merciless tactics of the Umayyad family created powerful opposition against them all, ending with the last caliph, who was assassinated in southern Egypt by the Abbasids, a rebel group loyal to Muhammad's family. The dynasty lasted ninety years.

The significance of this event is that it sets a precedent for Muslims to fight against a Muslim government if it is considered corrupt. The radicals say that the Abbasids carried out Allah's judgment against the Umayyads. They use the event to counter the argument that fighting against a Muslim brother is contrary to the teachings of the Quran, which only legitimized fighting against the enemies of Islam, such as Christians, Jews, and polytheists. So the radicals reason, "How are we supposed to fight those outside Islam when our homeland is being ruled by a religiously corrupt and misled group? In order to comply with the Quran, we must improve our internal affairs and erase all the agents working against Islam, even if they claim to be Muslims."

Now let's look at the next dynasty to see what kind of example the family of Muhammad will set for the Muslim world.

Abbasid State (A.H. 132–656/A.D. 750–1258)

The house of Muhammad, known as the Abbasid State, made complete destruction of the Muawiyya line their top priority after the Abbasid State took over the empire. The first caliph, Abu el Abbas, was known as "The Slaughterer," and he ordered his men to terminate any Umayyad living in the kingdom—man, woman, child, or elderly. They kept at it until there were none left except for two—Abdul Rahman and Salman.

Abdul Rahman had escaped to Spain, but the caliph had spared Salman because they had been childhood friends. This bond, however, proved to have a breaking point. Salman was eating lunch with the new caliph when one of the Abbasid poets came in and saw them sitting together and sharing food. The poet was enraged, and he stood up and recited poetry to the caliph, saying:

Do not be deceived by the looks of some people
For under the ribs, there grows a strong poison
Draw the sword, and take away your forgiveness (or pardon)
Until no Umayyad remains on the face of the earth.

The caliph smiled at his friend, took him into the next room, and killed him. This is the only incident in the history of Islam where a Muslim killed his Muslim brother for a couple of verses of poetry. When the Abbasids had no more foes to kill, they went to the graveyards, exhumed their bones, and crushed them.

This is the portrait of vengeance we receive from the cousins and descendants of Muhammad. I have given you these details to help you see the kind of legacy the Islamic radical discovers when he looks to the history of Islam.

Now let's see how the Abbasid State led to a powerful Islamic revival movement as well as the most influential revivalist of them all—Ibn Taymiyyah.

Internal and External Pressure Brings Religious Revival

During the Abbasids, the Islamic empire experienced many internal divisions that developed into independent states, such as the Fatimites and Mamluks in Egypt and the Jobians in Egypt, Syria, and northern Iraq.

There was a new external pressure as well that was caused by the Crusaders from Europe. Their continued attacks wrenched Jerusalem and the Holy Lands from Muslim control for a while, but those lands were later restored to the Islamic empire by Saladin the Jobian in A.D. 1187.

So while the internal struggle produced divisions, the external pressure of the Crusades produced powerful feelings of unity. When they felt they were being targeted, Muslims of all walks of life stood together. It became a period of revival, and they yearned for the early days of Islam. They wanted to pattern their lives after the victories and struggles of the prophet Muhammad.

They looked back to the Quran for guidance, for as Muslims say, it is the word of God, where "no wrong can come to it or because of it." In the Quran, they read, "Never will the Jews nor the Christians be pleased with you...till you follow their religion" (Surah 2:120), and in light of the Crusades they recognized these words as the reality for their daily lives.

The weakened Abbasid State finally succumbed to an invasion by the Mongols and dissolved in A.D. 1258. As the Muslims lived for the first time under foreign authority, the call to return to the roots of Islam continued. Ten years after the Mongols took over, Ibn Taymiyyah was born (A.H. 661/A.D. 1268). The next chapter will take you deep into this man's life, because he is the key link between today's radicals and the original teachings of Islam. You could say that he established the fundamentalist mind-set in his time, and the modern radical picked it up again.

16

IBN TAYMIYYAH: LINKING MUHAMMAD TO MODERN TIMES

At the time Ibn Taymiyyah was born, the Muslim world had experienced six and a half centuries of unrelenting bloodshed and fighting after the death of the prophet. Muhammad set the Muslims on this path, but people were tired of this miserable way of life. They became exposed to other ideas from the West, even through the interaction with the Crusaders. As a result, the Sufi sect of Islam became very popular.

Sufism is the most peaceful movement that has ever existed in the history of Islam. It focuses on the soul and the personality, challenging the Muslim to be a kind person and to establish peace with himself and others.

Sufis said that Islam did not require physical jihad. Instead, they said jihad was a spiritual struggle, that is, an inner struggle to follow the teachings of Islam. Muslims were ready for this position.

This chapter will trace the development of Sufism, Ibn Taymiyyah's fight against it and the Mongol conquerors, and how modern radicals are using Ibn Taymiyyah's teachings.

Rise of Sufism

Sufism was at its height during the time of Ibn Taymiyyah, yet you see the roots of this philosophy from the second century of Islam. The rise of Sufism can be described in three stages.

Stage 1

The philosophy of jihad put the early Muslim society in a position to never experience peace. Fighting, killing, spoils of war—these were the things the Muslims heard about the most. After relocating to Medina and gaining power, the prophet of Islam first ordered his military to submit all the tribes of Arabia to his ideology. After that their job was to move beyond the Arabian border to invade other countries, such as Egypt, the Eastern Roman Empire, and Persia (or Iran).

One of the most famous Muslims who began to preach about Sufi concepts was Al-Hasan al-Basri, who preached in the mosque of the city of Basra in the south part of Iraq. Al-Hasan al-Basri (A.H. 21–110/ A.D. 642–728) was the great imam philosopher/scholar of Sufism at the time.[1]

Even though Muhammad's conquest didn't go beyond Arabia during his life, his successors were able to put his plan in practice. The constant warring damaged the heart and soul of the Muslims. Many Muslims, especially in the second century of Islam, started searching for peace. They longed for reconciliation with others and reconciliation within themselves.

Another reason for the inner conflict was that by the second century, the Muslim army had conquered many people who were not Arabs. They had different backgrounds, different languages, and different mind-sets. For example, when Muslims took over countries like Egypt or Syria, they encountered the Christian lifestyle and the teachings of the New Testament.

They found Christian monks who lived in caves in the desert, avoiding the temptations of life, seeking peace for their souls, and establishing a closer relationship with God the Creator. That deep spirituality left a large influence upon the minds and hearts of some Muslim individuals who started to think for themselves.

Those who read Matthew 5 and 6 were greatly impacted. Some Muslims decided it was more important to them to win their souls and establish a relationship with Allah than to invade any country or get wealth by killing another human being. This is the root of the Sufism movement in Islam.

Stage 2

The second stage was the establishment of philosophy. In other words, how would Sufis interpret the Quran and hadith? How would they reconcile their peaceful philosophy with the physical jihad practiced by Muhammad?

The right person was needed, but this person wasn't a man as usual.

It was a Muslim woman named Rabi'a al-Adawiya (born between A.H. 95 and A.H. 99, about A.D. 717; died A.H. 185/A.D. 801) who lived in present-day Iraq.[2]

She was influenced by Christian monks in the Middle East who practiced Christian meditation. According to Islamic history, she was the first Muslim to speak freely about the love of Allah and to propose that Muslims should focus on the love of Allah, not the fear of Allah. This was a major philosophical development.

Stage 3

In the fifth, sixth, and seventh century of Islam, Sufism spread around the Islamic world and reached its maturity. When the Muslim world was invaded by the Crusaders, the Sufis were opposed to the use of force against them because they interpreted jihad as a spiritual struggle, not a physical struggle. This inevitably put the Sufis in conflict with orthodox Sunni scholars.

By the time the Mongols invaded the Islamic empire in 1258, the Sufism movement was at its height. However, a fiery scholar would change that.[3]

Ibn Taymiyyah: Following His Father's Footsteps

Ibn Taymiyyah (A.H. 661–728/A.D. 1263–1328) was born in Haran, a city in Eastern Syria near the Iraqi border, ten years after the Mongols invaded.[4] When Taymiyyah was six years old, his father relocated the family to get away from the Mongols. They traveled west and settled in Damascus, which was controlled by the Muslim Mamluks of Egypt. His father became an imam and a teacher in the mosque of Damascus as well as a famous scholar of hadith.

Ibn Taymiyyah pursued Islamic studies with his father as well as other famous scholars in the area. He was known to have a powerful memory, a sharp mind, and a strong will. He became a teacher, scholar, imam, preacher, and writer, and lived the first part of his life quietly, maintaining a good reputation.

However, he became outspoken on two topics (which we will review next) that would put him at odds with everyone—the Sufi Muslims, the Sunni Muslims, and the Mongol rulers.

Debating the Sufis

The first area of conflict for Ibn Taymiyyah was his relationship with the Sufi leaders. He began debating the famous imams of Sufism and became very aggressive against them. He objected to many of their teachings. For example, Sufism adopted a more Christian understanding of communication with God, similar to Jesus' prayer, "Let them be in Me as I am in You." So Sufis said that when they communicated with God, they would be united with Allah, and Allah would be united with them. Ibn Taymiyyah condemned this as absolute heresy.

He also condemned the Muslims for setting up shrines at grave sites and praying for the dead to beseech Allah on their behalf. Most of all, he objected to their reinterpretation of jihad.

Ibn Taymiyyah and his two disciples (Ibn Kathir and Ibn al-Kayim) were always debating the Sufi scholars and defeating them. They accused Sufism of being a Christian movement that had nothing to do with Islam.

Mongols accepting Islam

The Mongol elite began to convert to Islam, most significantly Gahzan-Khan, who ruled from 1295 to 1304.

Despite his conversion, the Mamluks continued to fight Gahzan Khan. In A.H. 699/A.D. 1300, when he was thirty-one years old, Ibn Taymiyyah joined the Muslim rebellion against the Mongols. He and other scholars traveled with the Islamic military and preached to them, encouraging them to engage in jihad against the enemy. Ibn Taymiyyah inspired them by saying their previous defeat was like Muhammad's defeat at the Battle of Uhud, but their current campaign would be like Muhammad's victory at the Battle of the Trench.

The Muslim caliphate defeated the Mongols in 1301, and Ibn Taymiyyah remained in the service of the Mamluks. In 1303, the Mamluk sultan asked Ibn Taymiyyah to give a fatwa (religious edict) legalizing jihad against the Mongols.[5] Taymiyyah's fatwa stated that it was the obligation of each Muslim to go to the battleground and respond to the call of war (jihad).

Radicals quote Taymiyyah often and always

The *Constitution of Al-Jihad* frequently quotes Ibn Taymiyyah, especially in reference to his fight with the Mongols. For example:

> The Sheik of Islam Ibn Taymiyyah says, "It has been proven by the Book and Sunna and the unanimity of the nation, that someone who deviates from one of the laws of Islam shall be fought even if he had spoken the two declarations (Shehadat)."
>
> Ibn Taymeyyah also said; "Faith is obedience, if some of it was in Allah and some was for other than Allah, fighting is a must until all faith will be in Allah."[6]

Muslim radical groups point to this fatwa and say, "This applies to us because we are living under rulers who claim to be Muslim but do not follow Islamic law completely." With Ibn Taymiyyah, they conclude that if a government refuses any part of Islamic law, then that government has chosen to follow man instead of Allah. Therefore, whether that government claims to be Muslim or not, it must be fought.

Defiant to the End

Ibn Taymiyyah believed in following the Quran whether it made people happy or not. In the year A.H. 720, the whole city of Damascus turned against him after he issued a fatwa in a divorce case and his fatwa wasn't supported by any of the four Muslim schools of Islamic law. He shocked them all by saying his ruling was based strictly on the Quran and hadith. He insisted on the fundamental mind-set, whether he was dealing with Sunnis or Sufis. He was tried, put in jail for five months, and ordered not to issue fatwas any longer. In defiance of that order, he made a fatwa in A.H. 726 to prohibit Muslims from visiting shrines at grave sites. He ran into big trouble again, especially after the discovery of one of his earlier books discussing the subject of this fatwa.

For Ibn Taymiyyah's safety, the governor of Damascus invited him to stay in the castle of Damascus. There Taymiyyah spent the rest of his life focused on writing until his death in A.H. 728/A.D. 1328 at the age of sixty. His ideas were carried on successfully by his two disciples—Ibn Kathir and Ibn al-Kayim.

The Significance of Ibn Taymiyyah

If you could ask a radical Muslim to describe the significance of Ibn Taymiyyah's life, he would say that he is a role model because he didn't do things to make people or leaders happy. He wasn't politically correct. He stood upon the Quran and the life of Muhammad alone.

Prior to Taymiyyah, the Muslims had been moving toward a

tolerant form of Islam. But then Ibn Taymiyyah and other scholars in this school of philosophy pulled the people back to the bloody ways of Muhammad, Abu Bakr, and Khalid ibn Walid. As a result, the Sufism movement almost disappeared. Today they represent less than five percent of the total Muslim population.

If there had been no Ibn Taymiyyah or if he had died as a child, the Muslim world today might have been dominated by Sufism and the global picture would be totally different.

Ibn Taymiyyah serves as a bridge that connects the modern time of Islam with the first century. He is directly responsible for returning Islam to its roots and establishing the fundamentalist mind-set.

Ibn Taymiyyah and the Blind Sheikh

I see many similarities between the blind sheikh, Dr. Omar Abdul Rahman, and Ibn Taymiyyah. The similarities are the commitment to the religion, the commitment to Allah, the prophet of Islam, and the Quran. It is also the commitment to do what is right for Allah, the prophet, and the Quran, not what is right in the eyes of the people or even what is right for the Muslim rulers in the Muslim lands.

Ibn Taymiyyah would issue a fatwa even if it would shock or cause trouble to the public because his only consideration was the application of Islamic law. He did nothing but present the true picture of Islam to the Muslim public through that type of fatwa. The public response didn't matter to him. Some received it with happy hearts while others spoke out against it and even tried to harm him.

The blind sheikh responds in the same manner. At one time he had a position as one of the famous scholars of Quranic interpretation at Al-Azhar University in Egypt. He didn't care about pleasing the public in the Islamic world, and he never thought to make the Egyptian government—or any other government—in the Islamic world happy. He never cared about his personal life or his position as a Muslim scholar and his job at Al-Azhar. But he chose to take the side of Allah and his prophet and try to bring the original Islam to the public through his fatwas.

The Ottoman Empire (A.D. 1301–1924)

During the life of Ibn Taymiyyah, the great Ottoman Empire was established. It survived for almost seven centuries and employed thirty-six caliphs. This empire completely destroyed the Eastern Roman Empire and took control of its capital, Constantinople (which is modern-day Istanbul), thus raising Muhammad's flag above one of the world's largest Christian cathedrals (Aya Sophia) and converting it into a mosque.

By the hands of the Ottomans, who conquered all the neighboring countries and attacked Europe from whichever way they could, the spirit of Muhammad became vibrant again. Islam was the dominant force in the world in those days.

Islamic radicals and youth sing a song about the glory days of the Ottoman Empire. The words are:

Muslims, Muslims, Muslims
Tolerant of death, refusing to give up.
For Allah's sake, how sweet it becomes.
By the sword we have overcome the mighty.
By the Quran, we enlightened life .
This is our history, oh you who ask.

Muslims, Muslims, Muslims
Ask history 'bout us, let it recall.
Who protected the rights of the weak?
Who built a better monument of glory?
I'll say, Muslims, Muslims, Muslims!

The locus of power did not shift until the Industrial Revolution started to take shape in Europe, commencing an era of Western colonial activities in the world. The Islamic world became a target for that activity.

We come now to another defining moment in history for all Muslims, and for the radical in particular. From the Muslim point of view, the West attacked the weakening Ottoman Empire with intellectual weapons, preaching freedom, democracy, and human rights. Finally, the end came, that grueling end for the Islamic world as a whole as the Ottoman regime collapsed in 1924 and washed away with it the Islamic caliphate, the system representing the political face of Islam.

The Modern Radical Movement

This environment produced the Great Awakening of Islam, led by the Founders, Hasan al-Banna and Sayyid Qutb in Egypt and Abul ala Mawdudi in India. The Founders were followed by the Evangelists, a younger generation of fiery writers who were ultimately executed by the Egyptian government for their crimes—Dr. Salah Sariah, Shokri Mustafa, and Abdul Salam Faraj. The third group of writers, the Prisoners (Abod Zoummar, Karam Zohdy, and Assim Abdul Maghed), was involved in the assassination of Sadat and imprisoned but not executed. A fascinating thing happened with the Prisoners. They stayed in prison for decades, and the first thing they did was write a passionate defense of the assassination. Then they led rebellion against the Egyptian government from inside prison. But they also had time to look at the results of their efforts (whereas other leaders were executed and never saw the long-term results of their activity). As a result they made some shocking changes in philosophy, which you will read about in the next chapter.

SECTION 6

HOPE FOR THE FUTURE

17

CALLING RADICALS TO CEASE-FIRE

When it comes to writing about Islamic radicalism, it is fairly easy to describe the problem. It is much more difficult to offer solutions. I wish I could offer a comprehensive military, political, social, and economic plan to solve the problem. However, I do have the ability to offer ideas for dealing with the religious and cultural factors of terrorism.

The purpose of the final section of this book is to present these ideas.

A Sign of Hope

A major development within radical Islam may point world leaders in the right direction to stop violence. The same men who authored the *Constitution of Al-Jihad* and who spent twenty-two years in prison (or more) have made an enormous change in their philosophy of jihad. If we can figure out why they made this change, there is hope that we can create the right environment for more radicals to follow their lead.

From 1992 to 1997, Al-Gama'a al-Islamiyyah spent five bloody years fighting to overthrow the Egyptian government. They attacked police officers, tourists, banks, and Christians. There was no negotiation with their philosophy. There was no way of appeasement. There was only fighting force with force.

At first, the police tried to eliminate radicals carefully, one by one. So if police heard of radicals living in a certain house, they would surround the house and call for the radicals to come out. In the ensuing firefights, many police lost their lives. As a result, after a few years, when police found out that a house had radicals, they didn't call for the radicals to come out. They just threw a bomb into the house and demolished it.

Egyptian President Mubarek arrested thousands of radicals and put them in prison where they were tortured.

Shocking announcement

During this time, the "historic leaders" of Al-Gama'a provided moral support from prison. Those leaders included Karam Zohdy, Assim Abdul Maghed, and Abod Zoummar, who had written the *Constitution of Al-Jihad* in 1986. But these leaders were feeling pressure. The group members outside of prison were being killed, and the group was no closer to their goal of taking over the government. Public opinion of the group was in a downward spiral as the nation suffered under the violence. Failure was inevitable.

During a military trial for one of their "brothers," these men and other Al-Gama'a leaders made a public statement on July 5, 1997, that shocked the Muslim world. In the courtroom, the defendant read an official statement from Al-Gama'a that called for Muslim radicals to end their violence and work toward a peaceful settlement with the Egyptian government.

What caused this change? Was it real or just a stall tactic? At first, most people, including the Egyptian government and other radicals, assumed the announcement was a ruse to gain a strategic advantage. Al-Jihad leaders in prison continued to maintain that their change was real.

An environment of hope

Although the leaders in prison called for a cease-fire, it took time for the entire group to accept this message. In a magazine interview, the prison leaders described the results of their announcement:

> Some Islamic radicals doubted that the statement was real. Others did not respond but waited to see what would happen. Even the Egyptian government did not respond at first... The "brothers" overseas rejected this statement, doubting that it was authentic.[1]

Even after the announcement some members of Al-Gama'a al-Islamiyyah in Egypt carried out an unauthorized attack. It was the infamous murder of fifty-eight tourists who were shot to death at the Hatshepsut Temple at Luxor in southern Egypt. Al-Zawahiri praised this attack in his later writings.

Call for peace survives

The call to end violence gradually gained momentum. Sheikh Omar Abdul Rahman, from his prison cell in the United States, issued a public statement in early November 1998 that called for the cessation of operations in Egypt and urged Al-Gama'a to create a "peaceful front."[2]

The death toll in Egypt dropped suddenly.

No terrorist-related deaths were reported in Egypt in 1999. That stands in contrast to the 1995 death toll at the height of the insurgency, which was 375. (About 1,200 people were killed in all during the campaign.[3]) In March 1999, group members outside the prison also adopted the cease-fire.

Thousands of Al-Gama'a members were still in prison (from the mass arrests following Sadat's assassination), but their conditions began to improve. *Al-Ahram Weekly* reported in 2002:

> The government, while vehemently denying that it had struck a deal with the armed group, began to improve its treatment of Al-Gama'a prisoners, ordering the release of at least five thousand to six thousand who had been detained without trial, or who had finished their sentences. There were also no further waves of administrative arrests of suspected members of Al-Gama'a, and to a great extent, reports of torture in prisons became fewer.[4]

By October 2003, the government had released almost one thousand Al-Gama'a members, including Karam Zohdy and Assim Abdul Maghed.[5]

The leaders wrote that the cease-fire was a "bridge that brought the people of Al-Gama'a al-Islamiyyah together to experience peace, forget the violence of the past, and focus on the main goal of preaching Islam and bringing Muslims back to their religion."

However, they took care to assure their followers that they did not forget their ultimate goal:

> We did not forget our main goal—victory for Islam. But wisdom is not to engage in endless war to destroy brothers and ourselves. If we continue with the violence, the end will be disaster.[6]

Unfortunately, not all parts of Al-Gama'a stayed in agreement with the cease-fire. Sheikh Omar Abdul Rahman rescinded his support in 2000. But what really matters now is that Al-Gama'a is not carrying out terrorist attacks in Egypt any longer.

How to Force a Cease-fire

Do you realize the significance of what occurred here? The philosophical leaders of a major terrorist group rejected violence and convinced many of their followers to do the same.

If we want to see the same thing happen in other parts of the world, then we need to know what happened in the minds of these leaders!

On June 19, 2002, the Egyptian government allowed them to address the public for the first time to explain the reasons behind the shift in their strategy. The result was a nineteen-page article in *Al-Mussawar*, the premier government-sponsored weekly magazine. Ironically, the editor in chief, Makram Mohamed Ahmed, himself a target of a failed Al-Gama'a assassination attempt in 1989, conducted the interviews.[7]

Karam Zohdy, the self-proclaimed leader of the movement, said that they changed their positions as a result of studying Islamic law. While in prison, Zohdy earned two law degrees, one from Cairo University.[8] Zohdy explained:

> Inside Al-Gama'a and other [Islamist] groups, some people know that we have revised our positions in accordance with Islamic Sharia (law) and found that killing civilians is prohibited. It is not right to rebel against the state at all. We, for example, have reviewed the issue of rebellion against the state with weapons, and we have found that there are many points barring and prohibiting such rebellion.[9]

Zohdy said that Al-Gama'a owes the Egyptian people "an apology for the crimes that [the group] has committed against Egypt."[10]

Zohdy also condemned the September 11 attacks against the United States by Al-Qaeda. "This event has badly damaged Islam and Muslims. Killing of innocent people is forbidden, and God will bring bin Laden to account for that."[11]

Another Al-Gama'a leader explained:

> Fighting is not in the interest of Islam and Muslims. The fighting which took place [in Egypt] split the nation, damaged the interests of society, and brought no advantage to the people. Therefore, it becomes meaningless, and prohibited under Islam, because it did not lead to guiding people to God's path, but rather caused a greater degeneration.[12]

In addition, these leaders issued several books explaining their new position. Their reported titles are:

- *Cease-fire*
- *Shining Light on the Mistakes of Holy War*
- *Declaring a Correction of Some of the Understanding of Mujahadin* (*Mujahadin* means people engaged in jihad.)
- *Prohibiting Extremism in Religion and Accusing Muslims with Apostasy*
- *River of Memories: Theological Revisions by the Islamic Society*
- *A New Jurisprudence for a Changing World: A Contemporary Outlook on the Issue of Divine Governance*

A New Path in Prison

The week following the magazine interview, the Egyptian government arranged for a gathering of five hundred Al-Gama'a prisoners to a specific prison where they attended a convention titled "A Cease-fire Initiative" led by Karam Zohdy as well as Najah Ibrahim, Ali Sharif, and Osama Hafez (June 2002). The front page of *Al-Mussawar* showed five hundred Islamists, bearded and dressed in white, holding a meeting inside the high-security prison.

The focus of the convention was Islam's view of the use of violence. Sharif told his fellow prisoners, "Our biggest mistake was our interpretation of Jihad and using this to kill civilians or tourists despite the fact that this is not the real meaning of Jihad in Islam."[13]

The leaders were asked a key question—whether the call for an end to Islamic insurgency attacks constituted a tactical or strategic change. Some Al-Gama'a members accused the leaders of changing their position in exchange for the government releasing them from prison. Zohdy responded: "An agreement with Jews can be temporary for a limited period until war against them is resumed. But in a peace agreement between Muslims there can be no exit."[14] In other words, Zohdy said that the cease-fire was permanent because it was made with Muslims.

River of Memories

With the cooperation of the Egyptian government, the radical leaders had the opportunity to explain their new philosophy in many ways. Their book *River of Memories* received the most media attention, and it showed just how much change had occurred in their philosophy. This book is a summary of discussions among Al-Gamaa's leaders and radicals over a period of ten months during their prison terms. Karam Zohdy, who had been imprisoned for twenty-two years, led the discussions. Key quotes from the book include:

> Egyptians should not shed the blood of Egyptians.... What happened was wrong and should not happen again.
>
> Women and children should not be killed, even in war.

The sheikhs called for "a complete and unconditional end to any act of violence, including verbal violence, against the Egyptian authorities inside or outside the country."

In reference to the killing of fifty-eight tourists in Luxor, Egypt, in 1997, they wrote: "In Luxor we killed men, women and children, young and old—innocent travelers who had come to visit our land.... It was wrong, wrong, wrong. Islam does not permit the murder of innocent civilians for any reason."

The sheikhs declared that they had misunderstood and misused the concept of jihad in Islam. They enumerated classical rules about jihad and declared that they had ignored these rules. They concluded that jihad could be interpreted as an order to war only if it is based on theological consensus, and even then only in self-defense.

They called for an end to armed struggle and a new strategy of re-Islamicizing Egyptian society through example and preaching. They described a campaign of "persuasion and encouragement" aimed at promoting "Islamic values."

Journalist Amir Taheri concluded that Al-Gama'a may have lost the military war, but it has exchanged it for a "political, social, and cultural war." At least the new battleground is not stained with blood.[15]

The degree of change for both the individuals and the group can hardly be overstated. A good example is Zohdy's comments about his role in Sadat's assassination.

In July 2003, Zohdy told a London-based Arabic newspaper (*Asharq al Awsat)* that Anwar Sadat "died a martyr during civil strife [*fitna*]." He said that if he could go back to the time of the assassination, he would "struggle to prevent it."[16] Those are amazing words from a man who previously described Sadat's assassination as ending "the life of that demon who spread corruption all over the earth."[17]

Interview With Hamdi Abdul Rahman

Why have these radical leaders renounced violence? Have their views changed significantly? What are their motives?

People all over the Middle East were asking the same questions. I had my own opinions about their motives, but I began searching for their response on Arabic Web sites. I found an amazing interview with Hamdi Abdul Rahman.[18] He is one of the top eight historic leaders of Al-Gama'a al-Islamiyyah. He joined with the historical leadership of Al-Gama'a to write the books explaining the group's new position against violence. After he was released from prison, he arranged to have the books published.

I couldn't believe that he or his peers would abandon their beliefs completely. And the interview proved that they did not, which means Al-Gama'a is still a dangerous group. But the interview does show what will force a radical group to look at a cease-fire as the best option according to Islamic law and history.

This is a big relief, because even a partial change in philosophy can stop the violence from these groups.

Let's look at how Hamdi explained their new position.

Hamdi's story

According to his interview, in 1974, Hamdi was a student at the school of engineering in Asyut University when one of his friends convinced him to establish a branch for Al-Gama'a al-Islamiyyah at Asyut University.

Hamdi said that the group chose to arm itself in the late 1970s because they saw how the government arrested and tortured members of the Muslim Brotherhood in the 1960s, and they wanted to be able to defend themselves against that happening to them.

Al-Gama'a and its splinter group, Al-Jihad, assassinated Sadat in 1981, but in reponse, the Egyptian government arrested thousands of them, including Hamdi, who was in his late twenties. From prison, they defiantly led a bloody campaign against the government. But at the same time, Hamdi said the leaders were reevaluating their thoughts, and reading and thinking deeply. "We put our hands on legal opinion that helped us change our thought, especially after we saw the result of the violence, how it affected Islam and Muslims and the country." After more than twenty years in prison and nearing the age of fifty, Hamdi and the other leaders called for a cease-fire.

The interviewer pointed out that some radicals look at the cease-fire as a step backward and a sign of instability in Al-Gama'a's belief. (Ayman al-Zawahiri, for example, is furious about what Hamdi and the other leaders are doing.) Hamdi responded with a very important point about Islamic law leaving room for change.

> There is no shame for us to change. Allah gave us our constitution [the Quran] and our law, and it will fit in different times and different positions. *That law gives us the right to change legal opinions according to the time and position of Muslims* [emphasis added].[19]

To further support this statement, Hamdi appealed to the concept of *nasikh*. *Nasikh* is the concept of progressive revelation, as demonstrated in the life of Muhammad. For example, at first Muhammad prohibited Muslims from visiting cemeteries, but later he allowed it. At first Muslims prayed facing Jerusalem, but later Muhammad changed the direction to Mecca.

Therefore, an older legal opinion can be superceded by a newer opinion based on a change in Muslims' circumstances or position. Hamdi said that the great scholars of Islam have changed opinions when needed, including imam el-Shafayen. This concept is important because it gives radical Muslims a dignified way to lay down arms and to pursue their goals through nonviolent means.

The interviewer then presented the biggest skepticism against the cease-fire—that it was a temporary strategy to allow Al-Gama'a an opportunity to build strength. Hamdi responded that the cease-fire was permanent because they had found legal opinions that prohibited rebelling against a Muslim government by using force.

He also explained that there was more than one reason behind the decision. He said that the leaders' study of Islamic law resulted in understanding five criteria for entering into jihad. The following are the five criteria he mentioned during the interview, followed by my comments based on information from *River of Memories.*

Five conditions in which Jihad is prohibited

1. Jihad is prohibited if it does not fulfill the criteria required by Islamic law.

Islamic law says, for example, that if the Islamic world has come under attack, Muslims who disagree with each other must put aside that disagreement and stand against the foreign attack.[20] At the time of the interview in February 2002, the leaders of Al-Gama'a perceived that the Muslim world was under attack due to the U.S. defeat of the Taliban in Afghanistan.

While the Muslim world is under attack, Hamdi stated:

> I see it as a must for all Muslims to be united in one body, no difference between ordinary Muslims or the Muslim governor or leader. All of them are targeted by foreign enemies, and we must protect our unity and stand in one line... to defend ourselves.

In other words, Hamdi perceived that the attack in Afghanistan was a threat to all Muslims; therefore, they needed to stop fighting each other and face the outside threat. Islamic radicals thought that the United States may continue to overthrow Muslim governments, and they wondered which one would be next. Hamdi's understanding of U.S. foreign policy was actually incorrect, but it served the unexpected purpose of creating a cease-fire against a Muslim government. It's a great illustration of an Arab proverb:

> My brother and me will fight my cousin. But my brother, my cousin, and I will stand together to fight the foreigner.

In other words, Muslims who are fighting each other will stop and stand together against what they perceive as a worldwide war against Islam. From their point of view, the non-Islamic world has attacked Muslims in their homeland, and it's time to go into survival mode. That is why many young men in Arabic countries have left countries, homes, and jobs and traveled to Iraq to fight against the coalition.

Unfortunately, the bottom line is that the cease-fire against the Egyptian government was motivated by a perceived need to stand together as Muslims against the West. However, other points of their logic call for restraint against attacking the West. (See 2, 3, 4, and 5.)

2. Jihad is prohibited if it conflicts with ***al-hidiya****, meaning "leading people to the good path."*

Al-hidiya keeps Muslims walking together on the same path, not confused and not neglecting their commitment to Islam. The opposite is *al-fitnah*, which means "to do something that puts people in a confused state." *Al-fitnah* causes people to wonder whether they should fight jihad or not. They question whether Al-Qaeda or Al-Gama'a is representing Islam or not. The Quran says, "Al-Fitnah is worse than killing" (Surah 2:191).

3. Jihad is prohibited if it will cause destruction or disaster for the Islamic world.

Al-Gama'a says that Osama bin Laden and his group are not using enough wisdom in their battle against the West; therefore, their actions have actually caused more harm to the Islamic world than good. For example, as a result of 9/11, the United States and others declared "war against terrorism," which is, in reality, war against Islamic radicals who practice terrorism. There had been a lull in Al-Qaeda's attacks against the West until suicide bombers attacked three subway locations and a bus in London on September 7, 2005. The reaction to this will be new determination in the West to shut down all means of support for Islamic radicalism.

Al-Qaeda is writing the final chapters of its story, and they will bring down other Islamic fundamentalists with them. Al-Gama'a condemned 9/11 and maintained their cease-fire with the Egyptian government to try to separate themselves from Al-Qaeda and to present a better image of Islam to the West.[21]

4. Jihad is prohibited if Muslims are captured by the infidels and the continuation of jihad (fighting) would put these Muslims in danger.

Before Osama bin Laden carried out his 9/11 plan, Al-Gama'a said he should have considered the result for Muslims living in the West. Would these attacks bring harm and danger to Muslims? Al-Gama'a says yes, an attack against the West harms Muslims in the West, and therefore, the attacks are prohibited by Islamic law.

5. Jihad is prohibited if Muslims are in a position of inability (not able to fight successfully).

Two conditions must be met before jihad can be declared:

1. Jihad must be for a specific reason, such as liberating a country from a foreign invasion or for taking over an infidel government and bringing back Islamic law.

2. Before declaring jihad, Muslims must achieve the specific level of power needed to reach their goal.

If these two conditions are not met, jihad has to be stopped because it wastes time, kills group members, and causes destruction without bringing any benefit to Islam.

When Osama bin Laden attacked the United States, culminating in the 9/11 event, he opened up a huge front with the West where he would not be able to achieve victory, said Al-Gama'a. Therefore, his 1998 fatwa declaring war against the "crusaders and Zionists" did not meet the requirements of Islamic law.

Analysis

Hamdi and his peers in leadership are doing a great service by explaining the reasons for their cease-fire. The question is: Can we stop worrying about them now, or are they still dangerous?

Here's what you need to know. These people are making their moves based upon *achieving* their goals, not upon *changing* their goals. In other words, Muhammad is still the perfect example for their walk and their lives. Quran and sunnah are still their source for belief, for disbelief, and for changing their minds.

This group found itself in a position where the superior power was on the side of the government. In addition, they had lost support among the public. They looked at how many years they had spent and whether the strategies they used were moving them toward achieving their goals, which are to establish an Islamic nation, restore Islamic law, and bring back the caliphate.

The question is: What to do? Continue the same way? If so, they will be demolished by the government. They looked back to history and asked, "Did any similar situation occur in Muhammad's life, and what did he do to preserve himself, his group, and his religion from destruction?"

For sure it happened in Muhammad's time when he became involved in a conflict with the Byzantine Empire (the Eastern Roman Empire) in Northern Syria. Muhammad sent an army of three thousand soldiers to fight an army of two hundred thousand soldiers from the Eastern Roman Empire. The Muslims were being slaughtered and their commander was killed. Another commander took his place during the battle, and the Muslim army continued to fight. The second commander was killed. Then a soldier named Khalid ibn Walid took over. He did not continue to fight. He called for a retreat and thereby rescued what remained of the army. If he had not retreated, the whole army would have been destroyed.

When the army returned, the people started to throw stones at them, accusing them of running away from the battlefield. Muhammad said, "I swear in the name of Allah, these people did not run away from the battlefield. They are good soldiers and fighters, but they had wisdom because they could not do any more there. They did not think of themselves or what people would say about them. They thought about how this would hurt Islam." This incident laid the foundation for the Islamic law that says jihad is prohibited if Muslims are in a position of inability.

So the radical Muslim concludes that if a confrontation with the enemies of Islam reaches a point where the battle would cause the destruction of the Muslim group, they have the right to lay down arms and retreat.

Did History Repeat Itself?

The path of Al-Gama'a is very similar to what happened to the Muslim Brotherhood three decades earlier.

The Muslim Brotherhood was established by preaching and spread dramatically in the 1960s. They tried to force President Gamel Nasser to apply Islamic law in Egypt. But he refused and reacted aggressively against the Muslim Brotherhood—even though he himself was a member of that group! They tried to assassinate him, and, in turn, he imprisoned, tortured, and killed thousands of them.

When Nasser died, Anwar Sadat took over. Sadat felt threatened by Communism in Egypt. He decided to support the Islamist groups and use them to demolish Communism in Egypt. In the 1970s he released many members of the Muslim Brotherhood from prison. He even allowed Sayyid Qutb's book *Milestones Along the Road* to be republished (even though Qutb had been executed for writing this book only a decade earlier).

After their release, members of the Muslim Brotherhood never spoke about violence anymore. Instead they taught that if you want to change the government, change the family first, then change the school, then change society, and ultimately the government will be changed. They said, "Start at the bottom and work your way up."

At this time, Al-Gama'a al-Islamiyyah was just a new baby. Though the Muslim Brotherhood tried to stop them, Al-Jihad chose to attack the government immediately, and they assassinated Egyptian President Anwar Sadat in 1981.

Vice President Hosni Mubarek took over and revived Nasser's method of controlling Islamist movements. Mubarek had thousands of members of Al-Gama'a arrested and imprisoned. While in prison, Al-Gama'a leaders began to move away from violent confrontation, just as the Muslim Brotherhood did in the 1960s. So they emerged from prison in the late 1990s with a new, nonviolent approach to achieving their goals.

The bottom line is that the Egyptian government survived by using overwhelming force against radicals. I certainly won't hold up the Egyptian government as a paragon of human rights and freedom, but we can learn principles from what has happened.

Applying These Ideas to Current Situations

The lessons learned from Al-Gama'a and the Muslim Brotherhood can be boiled down to a two-point strategy.

Point #1: Radical groups must reach the conclusion that violent campaigns will not achieve their goals and will lead to the destruction of their groups and their influence. In other words, radical groups must be answered with enough force and determination that they perceive a cease-fire as the only way for them to survive. This means that radicals' violence cannot go unanswered. Each unanswered act of violence makes them bolder. The *mujahadin* in Afghanistan felt that they could overcome a world superpower because they drove the Soviet Union out of the country. As Al-Qaeda moved on to attack U.S. interests overseas, the United States gave a weak response, which made Al-Qaeda bolder. They actually believe they could win an all-out battle with the United States.

If the governments of the world continue to demonstrate their military superiority and their resolve, radicals will eventually be forced to recognize that violence will not achieve their goals. Instead, violence will only succeed in self-annihilation and bring harm to the cause of Islam. In addition, the Muslim public will harden their hearts against radicals who continue to harm their society instead of improving it.

While it may not be possible to change the goal of Islamists, which is to claim the whole world for Islam, it is possible to cause them to change their current strategy of achieving it.

Al-Jihad stated in its constitution that "it is either a confrontation, jihad and fighting, or it is imprisonment, humiliation, and disgrace." The smart government will back radicals into a corner where jihad won't work and then give them a dignified third option: peaceful involvement in society.

Point #2: During the cease-fire, do not allow extremist groups to regroup and gather strength in order to make a better attempt at overthrowing infidel governments by force in the future.

It is possible that some groups will declare a cease-fire as a strategy of war. In other words, they will use the cease-fire as an opportunity to regroup and make better preparations to fight the next battle. Governments must cripple their ability to do this by:

1. Preventing radical groups from using funds for violent purposes.

2. Educating young people about teachings in the Quran and hadith that support spreading Islam through peaceful methods, not through jihad.

Some writers in the Muslim world have called this a "religious enlightenment campaign." Moderate voices need to be given a place within mass media, especially those controlled by government. In addition, these moderate voices need to have a prominent place on the Internet to counteract the thousands of Islamist Web sites that are feeding jihad to Muslim young men.

Perhaps the new writings of the historic leadership of Al-Gama'a can provide the philosophical foundation that a committed Muslim can follow to demonstrate the sincerity of his faith without causing harm to those who believe differently.

It is time for Muslim scholars and leaders to take the lead in educating Muslim society in an interpretation of the Quran that looks forward to the twenty-first century instead of dragging Muslim society backward into the seventh century. The next chapter describes the key areas of Muslim theology that need attention.

18
THE QURAN FOR THE TWENTY-FIRST CENTURY

To keep a weed from growing back, you must pull it up from the root. The root of Islamic terrorism is the fundamentalist application of the Quran and the life of Muhammad. Other factors—such as a poor economy and corrupt governments—are food and water that help the weed grow, and Islamic radicalism can be weakened by addressing those issues. But radicalism will not be kept under complete control until traditional Muslim society changes the way it interprets the Quran.

Seventh-Century Islam

When Muslims read the Quran literally and apply it to their lives, they are going backward into the seventh century. For some parts of the Quran, this method is fine. But there are many differences between the seventh century and the twenty-first century. The world today is not the world of Muhammad. The application of the Quran's teachings needs to take into account these differences.

Muslims need to interpret the Quran to fit with the twenty-first century. They need to make Islam a blessing to humanity, not destruction and disaster. Islam must build up human beings, not slaughter them.

If Muslims keep the classical interpretation of the Quran, they will never reconcile Islam with the rest of the world. The world will forever look at Islam with suspicious eyes and a lack of trust.

The new interpretation of the Quran needs to look at the teachings of Islam in light of the circumstances of the time of the revelation. If the circumstances that created the need for a particular teaching have changed, then the application of that teaching in the twenty-first century needs to change.

Just as Hamdi Abdul Rahman from Al-Jihad said, "[Islamic] law gives us the right to change legal opinions according to the time and position of Muslims."

Let's look at some areas where circumstances have changed for Muslims.

JIHAD IS NO LONGER NEEDED

The Islamic world needs to challenge the way radicals apply the teaching of jihad in Surahs 2, 5, 8, and 9. The fighting in these chapters needs to be seen as something done in the seventh century and no longer needed in modern times because Islam is in a totally different position than it was in the seventh century.

In the seventh century, Islam started as a small sect that was ridiculed by those with power. Now Islam is practiced freely all over the world. There is a Muslim World League with fifty-six nations as members. Even in most non-Muslim countries, Muslims are free to build mosques and worship and preach to nonbelievers.

The message of Islam no longer needs to be carried on the point of a sword because it can be published on the Internet, broadcast on television and radio, printed in books, and preached on the street corner.

The purpose of jihad was to preserve and advance Islam. But jihad in the twenty-first century does not preserve and advance Islam. Instead, it has put Islamic radicals in the crosshairs of the world military and police forces. Jihad has damaged the reputation of Islam worldwide. For the survival of Islam, jihad must be left in the past.

PREACHERS, NOT JUDGES

From the beginning, radical groups have justified their policies by declaring that Muslim society in general had become apostate. Muslim scholars have finally united against this accusation. Following is a quote from *Newsweek* regarding an historic meeting of sheikhs who issued a statement forbidding that any Muslim be declared *takfir* (apostate).

> The day before the London bombs, a conference of 180 top Muslim sheiks and imams, brought together under the auspices of Jordan's King Abdullah, issued a statement forbidding that any Muslim be declared takfir—an apostate.

> This is a frontal attack on Al-Qaeda's theological methods. Declaring someone takfir—and thus sanctioning his or her death—is a favorite tactic of bin Laden and his ally in Iraq, Abu Mussab al-Zarqawi.
>
> The conference's statement was endorsed by 10 fatwas from such big conservative scholars as Tantawi; Iraq's Grand Ayatollah Ali Sistani; Egypt's mufti, Ali Jumaa, and the influential Al-Jazeera TV-sheik, Yusuf al-Qaradawi. Signed by adherents of all schools of fiqh (Islamic jurisprudence), it also allows only qualified Muslim scholars to issue edicts.
>
> The Islamic Conference's statement, the first of its kind, is a rare show of unity among the religious establishment against terrorists and their scholarly allies.[1]

This kind of declaration is exactly what is needed. Muslims themselves are the best ones to challenge the ideology of the radicals.

Support the Voices of Moderation

Non-Muslims cannot try to tell the Muslim world how to interpret the Quran. Muslims who want to live peacefully with the world need to be at the forefront of this new interpretation. Too many Muslim Web sites are posting books by Hasan al-Banna, Mawdudi, and Sayyid Qutb. Instead, Muslim groups need to post materials by moderate Muslim scholars who write about tolerance of other people and beliefs.

For example, they should post the books by Dr. Farag Foda, who was assassinated by radicals for exposing the evil of radicalism and writing books to try to change their minds.

Moderate Muslims should help Muslim society grasp a clearer worldview. A good example is the writing of Anise Mansour, a liberal Muslim, who traveled around the world as a journalist and wrote many books. He served to connect Egyptian and Arab leaders with the rest of the world community. He did cultural exchange without judgment.

Leave Religious Education to the Family

The Muslim world has allowed its children to be indoctrinated through religious teaching that is far more fundamentalist and conservative than Muslim society in general. To help prevent the next generation of Muslim children from becoming radical, education in

Muslim countries should be totally secular. Let the parents guide their children's religious education.

Let the religious education belong to the family, and let the government schools be secular. The religious schools can't be shut down, but they need to be under watch.

Liberate the Muslim Woman

Women make up half of a society. When women are suppressed, it's like a body with only one leg functioning. The body is crippled and cannot accomplish as much as if both legs functioned. It is the same when Muslim women are not liberated. The Muslim society will not accomplish as much without their contribution.

The Quran's picture of women is based upon seventh-century circumstances. The Quran says the position of a woman is to stay in submission to her husband (Surah 2:223; 4:34). And Muhammad taught that the duty of the wife is to care for her husband's children, home, and wealth. She will be judged by how well she performs these duties.[2]

In the twenty-first century, a woman can fulfill the duties of Islam while at the same time pursuing an education, working at a job, or participating in politics. These options were not a possibility in Muhammad's time.

What keeps Muslim women trapped in their homes and hidden behind the *hijab* (the covering used to conceal a woman's body) is the literal application of some specific teachings in the Quran, such as:

> O Prophet! Tell your wives and your daughters and the women of the believers to draw their cloaks (veils) all over their bodies... That will be better, that they should be known (as free respectable women) so as not to be annoyed.
>
> —Surah 33:59 (see also Surah 24:31, 58ff)

> And stay in your houses, and do not display yourselves like that of the times of ignorance.
>
> —Surah 33:33

> And when you ask (his wives) for anything you want, ask them from behind a screen: that is purer for your hearts and for their hearts.
>
> —Surah 33:53

A twenty-first-century interpretation of the Quran would say that Allah asked women to do these things in the seventh century, but the circumstances of the twenty-first century are different, and women need not follow the seventh-century restrictions.

How will liberated women help stop radicalism? There are a few ways.

When women are confined to their houses by Islamic law, their contribution is lost for the economy, scholarship, and leadership. Society is weaker and more vulnerable to radical groups. When women are educated, participate in the work force, and have the right to vote in an election, they influence society for the better.

Women shape the next generation. Muslim women with little or no education do not have an accurate picture of the world to pass on to their children. This leaves children vulnerable to the intolerance and prejudice taught by radicals. Educated women pass on a more accurate picture of the world to their children.

Conclusion

The power of a new interpretation of the Quran lies in the fact that a Muslim can demonstrate commitment to his faith without destroying society. In other words, the fundamentalist interpretation of Islam requires Muslims to commit crimes to prove their commitment to Allah. The purpose of a new interpretation of the Quran is to show Muslims how to demonstrate full devotion to Islam while building up society instead of tearing it down.

Unfortunately, a fundamentalist Muslim is unlikely to accept a new interpretation of the Quran. He is only reasoned with by force. The benefit of a twenty-first-century interpretation of the Quran is to discourage new recruits from joining the radicals and to stop new radical groups from forming.

However, the Muslim understanding of his faith is not the only matter of religion to contend with. The world must also confront the Muslim understanding of other people's faiths. We need to "take religion out of the fight."

19

TAKE RELIGION OUT OF THE FIGHT

Imagine that you are a parent and you are raising your two children in a typical American neighborhood. However, all the time you tell your children, "Don't talk to the neighbors across the street. They are bad, ugly people. They hate you."

When your children go outside, they sometimes see the neighbors, and the neighbors never smile or say, "How are you?" Instead, the neighbors shout angrily at them and accuse them of causing trouble.

So the children decide, "Look—what our mom and dad told us is right. We should have nothing to do with these people." Their experience supported the teaching they received, and it became a living belief inside them.

In the Muslim world, this is the process whereby an entire society maintains a dangerously distorted picture about westerners, Christians, and their goals. A Muslim's understanding of Western religion—Christianity—clouds his perception of the West.

To challenge Pillar #5—faith is the reason—we must correct this distorted picture of Christianity and the West.

What Muslims Think About Christians and the West

An American who wants to dismiss something as old and irrelevant would say, "That's history." However, a Muslim would never say that. For him, the past and the present cannot be separated. His feelings about the past are as strong as his feelings about the present.

Muslims have events from 1,400 years ago as fresh in their minds as the news from last week. In their minds, Christians have been trying to destroy Islam since the time of Muhammad. They believe that all westerners are Christians, and all Christians are motivated with a desire to stamp out their religion. They point to proofs such as:

- The Eastern Roman Empire marched against Muhammad with two hundred thousand men and decimated the Muslim army of three thousand men (A.H. 8/A.D 630).
- Crusaders took Jerusalem from the Muslims, spilling blood in the Al-Aqsa Mosque (A.D. 1099).
- Napoleon Bonaparte invaded Egypt and Syria (1798–1801).
- America invaded Afghanistan (2001).
- America invaded Iraq (1991, 2003).

For Muslims, these are all the same event. There is no difference between the first crusade and America invading Iraq. In their minds, it's all about Christians trying to stamp out Islam.

Radicals are not the only Muslim group that feels this way. It is an opinion that permeates the entire society. A government-owned Egyptian national newspaper carried a column by a famous Egyptian scholar from Al-Azhar in February 2005 that read:

> The American government says "war against terrorism." It's not that simple. The real struggle we face today is bigger than that. It's not a struggle against a few terrorists, as they say. It's as simple as this: It's a struggle against the *faith* that is standing against the values and civilization of the West. The struggle against America is not a small struggle; it's an ideological struggle of *faith* (emphasis added).

This man looks at America as a Christian country that is leading a crusade against Islam. Whether Muslims are from Iraq or Indonesia, Arab or non-Arab, this is the way they think.

They have no idea that most of America is secular. They know their society is committed to its faith and assume that in a similar way all Americans are committed to Christianity and are ready to fight and die for its cause just as they are for Islam.

Their suspicions about Christians are confirmed when they hear Christian leaders criticize Islam. For example, when evangelical leader Jerry Falwell made some mildly critical comments about Muhammad on the television program *60 Minutes,* Muslims around the world protested. Some Shiite Muslim clerics in Lebanon and Iran, enraged by Falwell's comments, even called for his death. Falwell later apologized in an official statement, but for these Muslims, the apology came too late.[1]

Christians in Western society are used to having their faith criticized all the time, but criticism is a huge offense in the Muslim world. It is not forgiven or forgotten.

The Muslim View of Christianity

Did you realize that Muslims overseas watch Christian television programming? They have no idea that most Christians in America never turn on Christian TV. So they watch it, and they think they are seeing a window into Christianity. They see two different kinds of programming.

1. *The 700 Club,* Trinity Broadcasting Network/Benny Hinn style. Although these people may be sincere, to Muslims, they appear to be false prophets who are practicing magic. Muslims are offended by the makeup and clothing that the women wear and equate it to a nightclub scene. In their estimation, this Christianity could not possibly connect with the God of heaven.

2. Pat Robertson, John Hagee, Rod Parsley, and other Christian leaders. In their efforts to educate Christians about Islam, these Christian leaders appear to criticize and condemn Muslims. Muslims see them as the New Crusaders, stirring up Christians to attack Islam.

These kinds of things reinforce what the Muslims have been taught and believe from history. Muslims need to hear something from the Christian world that challenges their beliefs. They need to hear a message like this:

> We are brothers and sisters in humanity. Jesus died for the Muslims as He died for the entire world. God came with the plan of salvation for Muslims just as He did for the entire world. Muslims have been hurt by false teaching. It has separated them from us.
>
> We should model our prayer after Jacob, "I will not let you go unless you bless me..." (Gen. 32:26) and say, "Lord, I will not let You go until Your light shines before Muslims."

What would happen if Muslims see tears in Christians' eyes and ask, "Why are you crying?" and the Christians say, "We cry and pray for your sake."

Christians need to tell Muslims, "We disagree. But we declare our love."

Many people remember the story of Gracia and Martin Burnham, two American Christian missionaries in the Philippines who were kidnapped by a Filipino Muslim rebel group that later murdered Martin. The Philippine government has been fighting these Muslim rebel groups for years, and the rebels' hatred is fueled by what they perceive as an oppressive Christian government. But a Christian group called "Project ISLAM," an acronym for "I Sincerely Love All Muslims," founded by a Christian military officer, Col. Johnny Macanas, is helping to change the way Muslims feel toward Christians. By meeting the basic needs of Muslim residents, Project ISLAM is winning over the Philippine Muslims and changing hatred into love.[2]

Can Christians in general embrace the phrase: "I Sincerely Love All Muslims"? This is a much greater sacrifice for Christians in Muslim nations than it is for Christians in the West. The Christians in Muslim lands have lived under the attacks from Muslims for centuries while Christians in the West live in safety and protection. Yet Christians know that Jesus taught:

> But I tell you who hear me: Love your enemies, do good to those who hate you, bless those who curse you, pray for those who mistreat you.
>
> —LUKE 6:27–28

Jesus called for His followers to lay down the right to take revenge and to choose instead to love every person God has created—including all Muslims.

What Can Be Accomplished

Why is it important for the Christian community to unsettle the false picture of Christianity in the Muslim mind? How can this help the war against Islamic terrorism?

1. The Muslim world equates the West with Christianity (even though this picture is out of sync with reality).

2. The Muslim world believes that Christians hate Muslims and want to destroy Islam; therefore, they believe that the West hates Muslims and wants to destroy Islam.

3. Christians can challenge and change the Muslim beliefs about Christianity by speaking respectfully about Muslims, Muhammad, and Muslim beliefs; providing humanitarian aid to Muslims; and apologizing for offenses that Muslims feel have been committed against them by the church/the West (Crusades, colonialism, Muslims killed in Bosnia).

4. When the image of the church improves, the image of the West improves as well.

5. When Christians are "humanized" and are not the monsters of popular Muslim beliefs, it is harder for the Muslim public to support indiscriminate killing of "infidels" as carried out by Al-Qaeda and others.

A Word of Caution

A word of caution: Christians need to be "streetwise" about their relationship with Muslims. It's similar to someone from a small Midwest town going to visit New York City. He needs to learn some specific information about where to go and how to behave so that he does not put himself in harm's way. In the same way, Christians need to understand enough about the teachings of Islam that they do not put themselves in harm's way.

For example, people must show respect at all times toward Muhammad and the Quran. A printed copy of the Quran must be treated respectfully, never thrown on the floor or put underneath another book. Never say insulting words about Muhammad, such as he was a "thug," a "pedophile," or anything else of the kind. Among some Muslims, these poor choice of words can put you in danger of being beaten or even killed.

Another issue is that a Western Christian will see the surface similarities between Islam and Christianity and begin to think that perhaps both faiths worship the same God. It is easy to make this mistake if you learn only a little bit about Islam from someone who has an interest in making Islam look good to you. Therefore, Christians need to see the complete picture of Islam from its original source—the Quran and hadith. This is the purpose behind all the books I write. (For a very clear picture of the differences, you can read my book *Jesus and Muhammad.*)

Nevertheless, on a personal level, Christians and Muslims can be great friends.

Conclusion

The church can help show the Muslim world that America is not engaged in a religious battle. It is a battle about national security and politics, not about faith. Take religion out of the fight.

20

ENGAGE THE SILENT MUSLIM MAJORITY

When the media are filled with news of bloodshed and violence at the hands of Islamic radicals, it is easy to forget that radicals are a minute percentage of the Muslim community worldwide. That's because the moderate Muslim majority fails to speak out effectively against the radicals. To understand what keeps them silent, we need to see that the moderates can be divided into three groups:

1. Secular/ordinary
2. Liberal
3. Orthodox or traditional

Secular/Ordinary Muslims

The secular/ordinary Muslims are in the majority throughout the Islamic world. We can call them the "silent majority." They usually are not educated in Islam, and they don't have much understanding or knowledge about Islam as a religion, law, or history. The radical would call them "secular," but in reality they are simply ordinary.

Liberal Muslims

Liberal Muslims are usually well educated. Some are writers, journalists, businessmen, doctors, engineers, lawyers, and leaders in the local police or military. Usually most of these people have a very good understanding of Islam as a faith and a culture.

A good example of a liberal is Dr. Iyad Alawi, chosen to be the interim prime minister of Iraq in 2004, or other similar figures in the liberal movements in these countries. These people became liberal because they grew up in open-minded families and received secular educations, not religious educations. Most of them traveled to the West in completing their education or doing business. Usually these people don't allow Islamic teaching and culture to have a strong influence over their minds, and they have a big-picture view of humanity on a global scale.

Ordinary and liberal Muslims come together in one respect: their lack of interest in having their countries become Islamic states and apply Islamic law. In general, they would rather not see their nations fall into the hands of religious Muslim people.

ORTHODOX MUSLIMS

Orthodox people are stuck in the middle of the teaching and the culture of Islam. They don't have a humanitarian worldview. All they have is the orthodox Islamic view. They cannot see anything in life or in the world around them without the orthodox Islamic view.

For example, if you ask them, "What do you think about the incredible freedom that the West has given to women in their society? Look: today an African American woman is the secretary of state to the most supreme, powerful nation on earth [Condeleeza Rice for the United States]."

These people will answer: "It makes no difference to me if she is black or white. We, as Muslims, would never tolerate something like this. This is against the will of Allah and against the law of Islam. This is against the teaching of the prophet, and we know that the prophet said in the hadith, 'A nation who will put a woman in a high position will never succeed.'[1] The Quran also tells us in Surah 4 that man is superior above woman, and a man should be in a position like this, not a woman."

Orthodox Muslims are a source of new members for the different Muslim terrorist groups. Most orthodox Muslims have not yet joined the terrorist groups to practice jihad by fighting, but they still practice jihad in other ways. The Quran says Muslims can fight jihad:

- By physical fighting
- By giving money to the terrorist groups
- By words, if they cannot fight or give money

Don't ever think that only the people who are involved in terrorist groups are the terrorists. This is not correct. *Any* person who contributes *any effort* to the terrorist activity is a terrorist, too. He can give money, preach in the mosque that Muslims should join in the jihad, or speak in the media. Islamic law gives Muslims permission to practice jihad according to their ability.

How the Silent Majority Views Terrorism

The silent majority of Muslims knows very little about the teachings in the Quran and sunnah that give Muslims the right to use terrorist activity as a war method against the enemies of Islam. All they know about Islamic teaching on terrorism is the terrible, disgusting result of terrorist activity. They see what has happened recently in the West—the airplane attacks of 9/11; the bombing of the train in Madrid, Spain; the bombing of the subways and a bus in London—and they have experienced even greater evil in their own lands.

- In Iraq, Iraqis have experienced the kidnapping and killing of innocent men, women, and children.
- In Algeria, North Africa, terrorists have killed more than 150,000 Algerians in the conflict between the local government and the terrorists.
- In Egypt, during the government's conflict with Al-Jihad and Al-Gama'a al-Islamiyyah, thousands of innocent men and women lost their lives.

The hearts of the silent majority are troubled day and night when they see the news. The good news is that this silent majority does not supply new members for the terrorist groups. They usually want to live in peace with themselves and with others. They are busy with their lives, doing business, raising families.

The silent majority is completely involved in the present. They don't care to live in the past the way the orthodox do.

Living in the War Zone

I lived in Cairo, Egypt, during the conflict between the Muslim radical groups and the national government. When you walked on the streets, when you went to market, when you went to school, traveling by car or train from the south to the north, you could feel that the country was engaged in a war from the inside. You saw the increase of police officers in the public areas. You saw the increase of checkpoints at the entrance to cities.

That situation made life a living hell for the silent Muslim majority. They were frustrated, unhappy, and very angry with these terrorist groups. They could not understand why the members of these groups were killing their own Egyptian brothers who were police officers or government officials or even innocent bystanders.

If you asked this Muslim majority about what was going on, they would tell you, "The members of these groups are stupid, crazy young men who do not have full understanding of Islam. Islam does not agree with what they are doing. Allah, the God of Islam, and his prophet cannot be happy with what these people are doing."

The question is if the majority of Muslims are so frustrated with radicals, why don't they do more to stop them?

What Keeps the Silent Majority From Fighting Radicalism?

Most of these silent Muslims did nothing but watch the conflict between the radicals and the government. They watched and cursed. But the majority of them choose to be silent, not even to try to help the government or to assist the local police in catching these people. Why is this?

Fear of retribution

A person who contributes toward the fight against a radical group opens himself to the possibility of retribution. This retribution can come from different places. For example, the terrorist organization itself may find the collaborator and take revenge. Hamas, in Palestine, is famous for this. Or the collaborator may find himself in danger of "honor killing" from the captured radical's family, particularly if the family is large. "If you kill my brother, I kill you," according to a popular Arab saying.

Writers and journalists sometimes speak out against the radicals, but they put themselves in danger. An example is Farag Foda, who wrote books exposing the strategies of terrorists in Egypt. Radicals shot him to death in 1992. The second key example is the most famous writer in the Arabic world, Dr. Naguib Mahfouz, a 1998 Nobel Prize winner. He was seriously stabbed by radicals in 1994 but survived.

Culture of loyalty

Sometimes Muslim radicals are living in a neighborhood mostly populated with silent Muslims. The radicals may rent a house or live in a house that is owned by someone sympathetic to their cause. Unlike in the United States, in Islamic countries, a neighborhood is a close-knit community. The people living in the area will avoid speculating about whether their neighbors are radicals. They don't want to be suspicious of others in the neighborhood. They don't want to hurt each other. Reporting someone to the police goes against the culture. There are friendships, relationships, and history between people. They put those relationships above national security and helping the government.

Respect for radicals' commitment

Some of the silent majority are impressed that a group would be willing to fight and die for Allah. They feel guilty that they have not reached this high level of commitment personally. They think to themselves, *These are people of courage—whether their beliefs are right or wrong.* They wonder, *Maybe the radicals have the true picture of Islam. It would be better for me not to oppose them because I might anger Allah.*

Focus on personal needs

In many Muslim countries, life is hard, and the average people focus much of their energy on survival. They are working hard to raise their families and meet their needs. They don't see much advantage to speaking out against radicals and causing trouble for themselves. "I have no time for this; it is a government problem," they say. They will never go out on the street and demonstrate against terrorism.

How to Give a Voice to the Silent Majority

The silent majority lives in fear from dictators and radical groups. They need to be delivered from this fear. The number one way to give a voice to the silent majority is to give them security, democracy, and freedom.

Let's look at what has happened in Iraq up until the summer of 2005. The Iraqi people had been living under the dictatorship of Saddam Hussein and the fear of the radical Muslim groups inside the country who were fighting against Saddam's regime. After the invasion of Iraq, they were delivered from the fear of Saddam Hussein, and they are in the process of being delivered from the fear of the radical Muslim groups. The free Iraqi government and the coalition in Iraq will steadily target and eliminate these radical groups. These groups will not silence the majority in Iraq because they will not survive long enough to do it.

The people of Iraq are the most blessed people in the Islamic world because they have already achieved a large amount of human rights and freedoms. Iraq's silent majority has already walked more than halfway to the end of the road in achieving full and complete freedom.

If you want to see a glimpse of freedom, go to the BBC News (UK edition) Web site (under the heading "Middle East/Your Perspective") and read the opinions that Iraqi people write about the subject of the day. The Iraqi silent majority is silent no more. They speak in freedom and with power, discussing different subjects with no fear because they are living under a free government in a free country.

Hold on to Hope

The world is engaged in a great struggle to control Islamic radicalism, and the world will definitely win as long as it remains engaged in the fight. My hope is that the ideas in this book will help you see the picture clearly so that you can support the most effective ways of fighting terrorism.

EPILOGUE

Our journey into the mind of an Islamic terrorist is almost complete. However, I still need to fulfill my promise from chapter one to tell you rest of the story about my childhood friend, Kamal. You may remember that Kamal had joined Al-Gama'a al-Islamiyyah in high school, and he was part of the uprising in southern Egypt that was carried out in conjunction with the assassination of Egyptian President Sadat. The Egyptian government rounded up thousands of radicals at that time, including Kamal, and locked them up in prison under miserable conditions. Interrogation, intimidation, and torture were commonplace. After one year, Kamal was released and went home to his family in southern Egypt. He was a changed person.

In prison Kamal had shaved his beard, the symbol of his allegiance to the radical way of life. After he got out, he completely isolated himself from radicals and stopped going to their mosques.

I was still studying for my bachelor's degree at Al-Azhar University in Cairo, so I didn't see him. But I heard that he was struggling. Even though he had earned a bachelor's degree in chemical engineering, he couldn't get a job. No government agency would hire him because of his history of radicalism. He could not find a job in the private sector, either, so he was reduced to working at various odd jobs for the next two to three years.

Finally, he started looking for a job in the other Gulf countries, and he found one in Saudi Arabia. I did not realize, however, that somehow during this time, his wounded body and spirit had found peace in the teachings of Jesus Christ. In Saudi Arabia, Kamal met with members of an underground church. He also distributed some Christian pamphlets, which is probably how the Saudi Arabian religious police caught him. They sent him back to the Egyptian government, which put him in prison.

There is a huge irony here. Only a few years earlier Kamal was in prison for being an Islamic radical and participating in an armed revolt against the government. He had robbed many Christian businesses and pharmacies and killed their owners to raise money for jihad. Now he was in prison for converting from Islam to Christianity and handing out Christian pamphlets.

I cannot know exactly what happened to him in prison, but based on my personal experience, here is what I suspect. The prison officials interrogated him to find out how he became a Christian. I'm sure he was tortured in various ways. If he had denied the charges and said, "I am not a Christian," I believe they would have released him. But I suspect that he told them the truth and said he had left Islam to become a Christian.

After this confession, the police did not set up a trial and convict him of leaving Islam, because that is not a crime punishable by death according to official Egyptian law. But I suspect that prison guards—either on their own or following orders from higher up—took Islamic law into their own hands.

I heard the final news by telephone from my mother in Egypt because I was living in South Africa at the time. Sobbing, she told me, "They killed Kamal in prison by electric shock." She said that his father had refused to come to the prison to take his body because his son had become an apostate. So his brothers and some other friends came to get his body and buried him.

The news of Kamal's death hit me hard. I often thought, *It could have been me.* I too was arrested and interrogated in prison about converting to Christianity. Several times in prison I thought I would not live to see the next morning. However, the big difference with me was that I wasn't a Christian at the time. I could deny that I had converted and go free. But Kamal had truly chosen Christ, and he would not disown Christ (Matt. 10:32–34).

I dedicated the first book that I published in South Africa to my friend Kamal, with tears streaming down my cheeks as I wrote:

> To my beloved and faithful friend, Kamal,
>
> I love you, friend of my childhood. My heart weeps inside me for your departure. My only comfort is that you are now in heaven

> with Him whom you have loved and sacrificed your life for, the Lord Jesus Christ.
>
> Many write their life story with ink, and I am one of them. But few are those who write it with their own blood, and you are one of them. You came after me in the Christian faith, but you surpassed me by far.

Motive and Response

When I think about the life of my friend Kamal, I am so happy that he discovered peace and forgiveness before he died. Yet, I am so frustrated at the teachings of Islam that stole the joy of life away from him. For Kamal and all of Muslim society, I will continue to write and expose the teachings of Islam.

Here is how I hope you will respond to what you have read:

1. Separate

Please maintain a separation in your mind between the teachings of Islam and the Muslim community. The typical Muslim has no part in the ideology of the radicals. He is angry and frustrated by the radicals just like the rest of the world. Hatred and suspicion directed at the typical Muslim serves no good purpose.

2. Support

Now that Islamic terrorism has gone global, the world community must learn how to control it. A religiously motivated terrorist is not going to negotiate, and he's not going to be satisfied with partial concessions. On the other hand, world society is not going to accept *sharia* or a global Islamic caliphate. So the world must accept the inevitability of struggle against these groups and show a united front until the situation is under control.

3. Prevent

Even if the current group of radicals is put under control, a new generation will take their place unless steps are taken to change the environment that encourages radicalism. I don't know all the answers for this situation. But I do know that the faith factor cannot be ignored. Muslim society needs a twenty-first century interpretation of the Quran. The Muslim community itself must lead this change.

Thank You

To you, the reader of this book, I say thank you again for taking the time to go beyond *what* is happening and find out *why* it is happening. Your understanding is a great asset to the world community.

NOTES

Chapter 3—The Founders

1. Guilain Denoelcx, "Hasan al-Bana," Young Muslims in Pursuit of Allah's Pleasure, http://www.youngmuslims.ca/biographies/display.asp?ID=8 (accessed August 17, 2005).
2. Ibid.
3. A note to Western readers: You may have a hard time pronouncing *Qutb*. Think of the *q* as making a *ck* sound. Then think of the *u* as making the vowel sound in "foot." Then blend the *t* and *b* together as quickly as you can. You will hear a slight short *e* sound in between the two consonants.
4. Ahmed El-Kadi, MD, "Sayyid Qutb," Muslim American Society, Minnesota Chapter, http://www.masmn.org/documents/Biographies/20th_Century/Sayyid_Qutb.htm (accessed February 21, 2005). Wikipedia: The Free Encyclopedia, s.v. "Sayyid Qutb," http://en.wikipedia.org/wiki/Qutb (accessed February 21, 2005).
5. Lawrence Wright, "The Man Behind bin Laden: How an Egyptian Doctor Became a Master of Terror" (II—The Martyr), *The New Yorker*, September 16, 2002, posted on NewYorker.com September 9, 2002, http://www.newyorker.com/fact/content?020916fa_fact2b (accessed August 18, 2005).
6. "Sayyid Qutb's America: Al-Qaeda Inspiration Denounced U.S. Greed, Sexuality," *All Things Considered*, National Public Radio (NPR), May 6, 2003, http://www.npr.org/templates/story/story.php?storyId=1253796 (accessed September 8, 2005).
7. El-Kadi, MD, "Sayyid Qutb," http://www.masmn.org/documents/Biographies/20th_Century/Sayyid_Qutb.htm (accessed August 18, 2005).
8. Sayyid Qutb, *Milestones Along the Road* (Delhi: Markazi Maktaba Islami, n.d.), 12.
9. Wikipedia: The Free Encyclopedia, s.v. "*jahiliyyah*," http://en.wikipedia.org/wiki/Jahiliyyah (accessed August 19, 2005).
10. Trevor Stanley, "Maulana Maududi: Radical Islam's Missing Link," Perspectives on World History and Current Events, www.pwhce.org/maududi.html (accessed July 8, 2005).

Chapter 4—The Evangelists

1. Gilles Kepel, *Muslim Extremism in Egypt* (Berkeley and Los Angeles, CA: University of California Press, 2003), 93. This book was first published in Paris in 1984.

2. Dr. Salah Sariah, *The Message of Faith* (1973), in Rifaat Sayed Ahmed, *The Armed Prophet* (London: Riad El-Rayyes Books, 1991), trans. by Habib Srouji, November 2004.
3. Ibid.
4. Abdelwahab El-Affendi, "Hizb al-Tahrir: the paradox of a very British party," *The Daily Star*, September 3, 2003, http://www.aljazeerah.info/Opinion%20editorials/2003%20Opinion%20Editorials/September/2%20o/Hizb%20al-Tahrir,%20the%20paradox%20of%20a%20very%20British%20party%20Abdelwahab%20El-Affendi.htm (accessed September 20, 2005).
5. Arabic Web site labeled as the "media office of Hizb-ut-Tahrir," author's translation, http://www.hizb-ut-tahrir.info/arabic/index.php/main/index.
6. Trevor Stanley, "Shukri Mustafa: Spiritual Leader of Takfir wal-Hijra (Jama'at al-Muslimun) during the 1970s," Perspectives on World History and Current Events, www.pwhce.org/shukri.html (accessed August 19, 2005).
7. Zohurul Bari, *Re-Emergence of the Muslim Brothers in Egypt* (Lancer's Books: New Delhi, India, 1995), 70–71, as quoted by Trevor Stanley at www.pwha.org.
8. Shokri Moustafa, *El-Tawaseemat* [Expectation] (Cairo, Egypt: Shorouk International, n.d.).
9. Kepel, *Muslim Extremism in Egypt*, 59.
10. Ibid., especially chapter 3, "The Society of Muslims," as quoted by Stanley, "Shukri Mustafa: Spiritual leader of Takfir wal-Hijra (Jama'at al-Muslimun) during the 1970s."
11. Martin Bright, et al., Focus, "The Secret War: Part 2," *The Observer*, Sunday, September 30, 2001, http://observer.guardian.co.uk/focus/story/0,,560658,00.html (accessed September 20, 2005).
12. Sourcing for this section on Abdul Salam Faraj include: Trevor Stanley, "Muhammad Abd al-Salam Faraj: Founder of Jama'at Al-Jihad, the Group That Killed Anwar Sadat," Perspectives on World History and Current Events, http://www.pwhce.org/faraj.html (accessed May 22, 2005). Angelfire.com, "Biographies of Some Islamic Fundamentalist Leaders." Marc Erikson, "Islamism, Fascism and Terrorism (Part 4)," *Asia Times*, 5 December 2002, http://www.hartford-hwp.com/archives/27b/083.html (accessed September 27, 2005). "Faraj and the Neglected [Abandoned] Duty: Interview with Professor Johannes J. G. Jansen," interviewed by Jean-François Mayer in Amsterdam, December 8, 2001; transcribed by Nancy Grivel-Burke; http://www.religioscope.com/info/dossiers/textislamism/faraj_jansen.htm (accessed September 27, 2005).

13. Abdul Salam Faraj, "Fear of Failure," *The Abandoned Duty*, in Ahmed, *The Armed Prophet.*
14. Faraj, "The Clarification That the Nation of Islam Is Different From All Other Nations," *The Abandoned Duty*, in Ahmed, *The Armed Prophet.*
15. Mark A. Gabriel, *Islam and Terrorism* (Lake Mary, FL: Charisma House, 2002), 151–154.
16. U.S. Department of State, "Patterns of Global Terrorism," released by the office of the coordinator for counterterrorism, April 29, 2004, http://www.state.gov/s/ct/rls/pgtrpt/2003 (accessed Spring 2005).
17. Heba Saleh, "Egypt Hails Militants' Truce," BBC News World Edition online, July 13, 2002, http://news.bbc.co.uk/1/hi/world/middle_east/2126747.stm (accessed August 23, 2005).

Chapter 5—The Prisoners

1. Amira Howeidy, "Zero Tolerance for Torture," *Al-Ahram Weekly Online*, June 30 to July 6, 2005, issue 749, http://weekly.ahram.org.eg/2005/749/eg7.htm (accessed August 22, 2005).
2. Abod Zoummar, *The Strategy of Al-Jihad*, in Ahmed, *The Armed Prophet.*
3. Karam Zohdy, Assim Abdul Maghed, and Abod Zoummar, "Our Path and Our Way," from the Introduction of *Constitution of Al-Jihad* (issued 1987), in Ahmed, *The Armed Prophet.*
4. Oklahoma City National Memorial Institute for the Prevention of Terrorism (MIPT), Terrorism Knowledge Base, Egypt, http://www.tkb.org/Country.jsp?countryCd=EG (accessed September 22, 2005). Go to "Patterns of Global Terrorism" and click on the "overview" for the years 1992–1997.

Chapter 6—The Aristocrats

1. Sources for this chart include the following: "Osama bin Laden FAQ," http://www.msnbc.com/news/627355.asp (accessed September 27, 2005). Anonymous, "A Biography of Osama bin Laden," *Frontline*, www.pbs.org/wgbh/pages/frontline/shows/binladen/who/bio.html (accessed September 27, 2005). Dr. Nimrod Raphaeli, "Ayman Muhammad Rabi' Al-Zawahiri: The Making of an Arch Terrorist," *Terrorism and Political Violence*, vol. 14, no. 4, Winter 2002, http://www.jewishvirtuallibrary.org/jsource/biography/Zawahiri.html (accessed September 27, 2005). "Osama bin Laden Timeline," CNN.com, http://www.cnn.com/CNN/Programs/people/shows/binladen/timeline.html (accessed September 27, 2005). Jane Mayer, "The House of bin Laden: A Family's, and a

Nation's, Divided Loyalties," *The New Yorker*, November 12, 2001, http://www.newyorker.com/fact/content/?011112fa_FACT3 (accessed September 27, 2005).
2. Raphaeli, "Ayman Muhammad Rabi al-Zawahiri."
3. Trevor Stanley, "Abdullah Azzah: The Godfather of Jihad," *Perspectives on World History and Current Events: Middle East Project*, http://www .pwhce.org/azzam.html (accessed September 21, 2005).
4. Anonymous, "A Biography of Osama bin Laden," www.pbs.org/wgbh/pages/frontline/shows/binladen/who/bio.html.
5. Wright, "The Man Behind bin Laden."
6. Biography of Ayman al-Zawahiri from the Web site of The Pulpit of Monotheism and Jihad, the radical group headed by al-Zarqawi in Iraq and affiliated with Al-Qaeda, www.tawhed.ws/a?i=24 (accessed September 8, 2005), author's translation.
7. "Ayman Zawahiri: Last Will and Testament," first appearing in the London and Middle East Newspaper and posted on the Web site of the American Coptic Association, www.amcoptic.com/a_news/news_egypt/ayman_awahry_book.htm, author's translation.
8. Wright, "The Man Behind bin Laden."
9. Ibid.
10. Biography of Ayman al-Zawahiri, The Pulpit of Monotheism and Jihad, www.tawhed.ws/a?i=24.
11. Wright, "The Man Behind bin Laden."
12. "Osama bin Laden: A Chronology of His Political Life," *Frontline*, http://www.pbs.org/wgbh/pages/frontline/shows/binladen/etc/cron .html (accessed September 22, 2005).
13. Wright, "The Man Behind bin Laden."
14. Wikipedia: The Free Encyclopedia, s.v. "Gulf War: Casualties During the War," http://en.wikipedia.org/wiki/Gulf_war#Casualties_During_the_War (accessed August 23, 2005).
15. "Full Text: Bin Laden's 'Letter to America,'" *Observer* Worldview Extra, November 24, 2002, http://observer.guardian.co.uk/worldview/story/0,11581,845725,00.html (accessed September 22, 2005).
16. Wright, "The Man Behind bin Laden."
17. *Al-Fatawa* by Ibn Taymiyyah, vol. 28, p. 540 as quoted in Ayman al-Zawahiri, *Healing of the Breast of the Believers*, author's translation.
18. *Sahih Muslim* [The Correct Books of Muslim], Book 20, Number 4681, narrated on the authority of 'Abdullah b. Qais, who heard it from his father (It is #1902 in the Arabic version of the hadith of Muslim); English translation by Abdul Hamid Siddiqui; http://www .usc.edu/dept/MSA/fundamentals/hadithsunnah/muslim/020.smt.

html (accessed September 28, 2005).

19. Walter Pincus, "Zawahiri Urged Al Qaeda to Let Fighters Escape for Jihad's Sake," *Washington Post*, January 1, 2002, A13; available online at www.washingtonpost.com/ac2/wp-dyn/A46577-2001Dec31?language=printer (accessed September 22, 2005).
20. Al-Zawahiri, *Healing the Breasts of the Believers*, author's translation. The story of the capture of Ta'if is told in the English translation of Ibn Ishaq, *The Life of Muhammad*, trans. A. Guillame (Karachi, Pakistan: Ameena Saiyad, Oxford University Press, 2003), 587–592.
21. Robert F. Worth, et al., "Multiple Attacks Kill Nearly 150 in Iraqi Capital," *New York Times*, September 15, 2005, A1; www.nytimes.com (accessed September 15, 2005),

Chapter 7—Pillar 1: No Law but Islamic Law

1. Ibn Kathir, *Quranic Commentary*, vol. 1, pt. 2, page 213. As a student of Islamic history, part of my education was to memorize this story. Many hadith give this story in slightly different variations. In fact, the version I memorized said that one of the men in the story was a Jew. But because I cannot find that version in the sources I have available to me in the United States, I will give you the story as historian Ibn Kathir told it.
2. Qutb, *Milestones Along the Road*, 107–108 (chapter 4).
3. Ibid., 107–108, 144. See also Surah 12:40; 42:21.
4. Ibid., 108.
5. Sayyid Abul ala Mawdudi, *Jihad in Islam* (Lahore, Pakistan: Islamic Publications), 14; http://www.islamistwatch.org/texts/maududi/maududi.html (downloaded July 2005).
6. James G. Lochtefeld, "The Formation of the *Shari'a* (Islamic Law)," Material Sources for the Shari'a, http://www2.carthage.edu/~lochtefe/islam/sharia.html (accessed March 14, 2004).
7. Qutb, *Milestones Along the Road*, 157. *Ijtihad* can be done by a single scholar, whereas *ijma'ah* derives from the group consensus.
8. Ibid., 167.
9. Non-Muslims may have a hard time believing that Muhammad really commanded his followers to kill any person who professes Islam and then turns away. However, this saying of Muhammad is clearly recorded in *Sahih al-Bukhari* [The Correct Books of Bukhari], Volume 9, Book 84, Number 57, English translation by Dr. Muhammad Muhasin Khan, which you can read on the University of Southern California Web site: http://www.usc.edu/dept/MSA/fundamentals/hadithsunnah/bukhari/084.sbt.html#009.084.057

(accessed September 28, 2005).

10. *Sahih Muslim* [The Correct Books of Muslim], Book 17, Number 4226, http://www.usc.edu/dept/MSA/fundamentals/hadithsunnah/muslim/017.smt.html (accessed September 28, 2005).
11. *Sahih al-Bukhari* [The Correct Books of Bukhari], Volume 8, Book 81, Number 778, http://www.usc.edu/dept/MSA/fundamentals/hadithsunnah/bukhari/081.sbt.html#0089.081.778 (accessed September 28, 2005).
12. Qutb, *Milestones Along the Road*, 110.
13. Mawdudi, *Jihad in Islam*, 28.
14. Sariah, "Faith in Allah," *The Message of Faith*, in Ahmed, *The Armed Prophet*.
15. Sariah, "The Governing Body," *The Message of Faith*, in Ahmed, *The Armed Prophet*.
16. "Sharia for Canada?", program transcript of *The Religion Report* with David Rutledge, Radio National, 2 February 2005, with guests Syed Mumtaz Ali and Alia Hogben, http://www.abc.net.au/rn/talks/8.30/relrpt/stories/s1334120.htm (accessed September 9, 2005).

Chapter 8—Pillar 2: Infidels Are All Around

1. Qutb, *Milestones Along the Road*, 148.
2. Sariah, "Objectors to the Islamic Laws," *The Message of Faith*, in Ahmed, *The Armed Prophet*.
3. Faraj, "Today's Rulers Are in a Retreat Away From Islam," *The Abandoned Duty*, in Ahmed, *The Armed Prophet*.
4. Ibid.
5. Zohdy, Maghed, and Zoummar, *Constitution of Al-Jihad* (issued 1987), in Ahmed, *The Armed Prophet*, emphasis added.
6. Ibid., emphasis added.
7. Faraj, *The Abandoned Duty*, in Ahmed, *The Armed Prophet*.
8. Sariah, "The Preconditions for Apostasy," *The Message of Faith*, in Ahmed, *The Armed Prophet*.
9. Qutb, *Milestones Along the Road*, 155.
10. Ibid., 247.
11. Ibid., 245.
12. The Fatwa of Ibn Taymiyyah, page 298, query number 217, in Faraj, *The Abandoned Duty*, in Ahmed, *The Armed Prophet*.
13. Zohdy, Maghed, and Zoummar, "First: Overturning the Immoral Ruler Who Alters the Commands of Allah," *Constitution of Al-Jihad*, in Ahmed, *The Armed Prophet*.
14. Islamonline.net in Arabic, under the page titled "Ask the Expert,"

under the question that reads, "Mahmoud from Jordan asked, 'What is the meaning of *Dar-ul-Islam* and *Dar-ul-Harb*?'"

15. Qutb, *Milestones Along the Road*, 221.
16. Ibid., 223.
17. Ibid., 234.
18. Ibid., 213.
19. Ibid., 217.

Chapter 9—Pillar 3: Islam Must Rule

1. Zohdy, Maghed, and Zoummar, *Constitution of Al-Jihad*, in Ahmed, *The Armed Prophet.*
2. Zohdy, Maghed, and Zoummar, "The Caliphate Over Fourteen Centuries," *Constitution of Al-Jihad*, in Ahmed, *The Armed Prophet.*
3. Ibid.
4. Qutb, *Milestones Along the Road*, 137.
5. Mawdudi, *Jihad in Islam*, 9.
6. Qutb, *Milestones Along the Road*, 238.

Chapter 10—Pillar 4: Jihad Is the Only Way to Win

1. Ibn Qayyim as quoted in Qutb, *Milestones Along the Road*, 94–95.
2. Qutb, *Milestones Along the Road*, 100.
3. Al Hafeth Mohammad Bin Ahmad Bin Mohammad Bin Jazi Al Kalbi, *Tafseer Al Tasheel, Li-Oloum Al Tanzeel* [The Simple Explanation of the Heavenly Knowledge], in Faraj, *The Abandoned Duty*, in Ahmed, *The Armed Prophet.* Faraj quoted many other scholars who gave the same explanation for the verse of the sword.
4. Zohdy, Maghed, and Zoummar, "Fourth Inevitability of Confrontation," *Constitution of Al-Jihad*, in Ahmed, *The Armed Prophet.*
5. Zohdy, Maghed, and Zoummar, "Where Is Palestine Today?," *Constitution of Al-Jihad*, in Ahmed, *The Armed Prophet.*
6. Ibn Kathir, *The Beginning and the End*, vol. 2, pt. 3 (Beirut, Lebanon: The Revival of the Arabic Tradition Publishing House, 2001), 53.
7. Zohdy, Maghed, and Zoummar, *Constitution of Al-Jihad*, in Ahmed, *The Armed Prophet.*
8. Ibn Hisham, *The Life of Muhammad*, 3rd edition (Beirut, Lebanon: Dar-al-Jil, 1998), vol 3., pt. 6, p. 8; author's translation.
9. Al-Ghazali, *The Revival of Religious Science* (Beirut, Lebanon: Dar al-Maharifa), vol. 1, p. 172. Al-Ghazali lived in the twelfth century and was the founder of the Islamic Sufism movement. His book did not list the primary source for this anecdote.

10. Faraj, "Categories of Jihad, Not Stages," *The Abandoned Duty,* in Ahmed, *The Armed Prophet.*
11. Ibid.
12. Qutb, *Milestones Along the Road,* 112–113.
13. Ibid., 134.
14. Ibid., 109.
15. Faraj, "Fighting Now Is an Obligation Upon All Muslims," *The Abandoned Duty,* in Ahmed, *The Armed Prophet.*
16. Qutb, *Milestones Along the Road,* 110.

Chapter 11—Pillar 5: Faith Is the Reason

1. Sariah, "Faith in Allah," *The Message of Faith,* in Ahmed, *The Armed Prophet.*
2. Sariah, "Believing in Fate," *The Message of Faith,* in Ahmed, *The Armed Prophet.*
3. Sariah, "Believing in the Last Day," *The Message of Faith,* in Ahmed, *The Armed Prophet.*
4. Ibid.
5. Ibid. See also *Sahih al-Bukhari* [The Correct Books of Bukhari], Volume 7, Book 70, Number 577.
6. *Sahih al-Bukhari* [The Correct Books of Bukhari], Volume 1, Book 2, Number 35, narrated Abu Huraira, http://www.usc.edu/dept/MSA/fundamentals/hadithsunnah/bukhari/002.sbt.html (accessed September 28, 2005).
7. Sariah, "Believing in the Last Day," *The Message of Faith,* in Ahmed, *The Armed Prophet.*
8. Qutb, *Milestones Along the Road,* 274.
9. Ibid., 295–296.
10. Ibid., 275.
11. Ibid., 276.
12. Ibid., 302.
13. Ibid., 55.
14. Ibid., 7.

Chapter 12—Deception: An Art of War Practiced by Radicals

1. *Sahih al-Bukhari* [The Correct Books of Bukhari], Volume 4, Book 52, Number 268, narrated Abu Huraira; also Volume 4, Book 52, Number 269, narrated Jabir bin 'Abdullah; http://www.usc.edu/dept/MSA/fundamentals/hadithsunnah/bukhari/052.sbt.html (accessed September 28, 2005).

2. From the hadith narrated by Um-Koulthoum, as quoted in Mussallam, *Revival of Religious Sciences,* 3–137, author's translation. See also the hadith narrated by Al-Noas bin Semaan.
3. Ibn Taymiyyah, *The Ironclad Sword Drawn Against the Messenger's Reviler* (N.p.: n.d.), 21, author's translation.
4. Ibn Kathir, *The Beginning and the End.* This is a massive work that described the history of the world from the Islamic point of view, starting with creation and ending just before the author's death in A.H. 774.
5. Al Mansour, *The Pleasant and the Wicked* (N.p.: n.d.), 199.
6. Mohammed Hasanayn Hakel, *The Anger of Autumn* (Cairo: Medbouli Publishing).
7. Faraj, "Deception of the Infidels Is an Art of War," *The Abandoned Duty,* in Ahmed, *The Armed Prophet.*

Chapter 13—Al-Zawahiri's Teachings on Deceit

1. *Sahih Muslim* [The Correct Books of Muslim], Book 30, Number 5848, http://www.usc.edu/dept/MSA/fundamentals/hadithsunnah/muslim/030.smt.html (accessed September 28, 2005).
2. *Sahih al-Bukhari* in Arabic, #3522, quoted by al-Zawahiri.
3. *Sahih Muslim* [The Correct Books of Muslim], Book 1, Number 0275 (in English), http://www.usc.edu/dept/MSA/fundamentals/hadithsunnah/muslim/001.smt.html (accessed September 28, 2005). Narrated by Muslim in the Book of Faith, vol. 2, p 179 in Arabic. Chapter 68 of the hadith of Muslim is titled "Permissibility of Concealing the Faith of One Who Fears."
4. Ibn Kudami al-Hanbali, *Al Mogny* [Satisfaction], vol. 1, p. 660. This is a book of hadith and law.
5. *Sahih al-Bukhari* [The Correct Books of Bukhari], Volume 4, Book 52, Number 198, narrated Ka'b bin Malik, http://www.usc.edu/dept/MSA/fundamentals/hadithsunnah/bukhari/052.sbt.html (accessed September 28, 2005).
6. *Sahih al-Bukhari* [The Correct Books of Bukhari], Volume 4, Book 52, Number 281, narrated Abu Huraira, http://www.usc.edu/dept/MSA/fundamentals/hadithsunnah/bukhari/052.sbt.html (accessed September 28, 2005).
7. *Sahih al-Bukhari* [The Correct Books of Bukhari], Volume 4, Book 52, Number 286, narrated Salama bin Al-Akwa, http://www.usc.edu/dept/MSA/fundamentals/hadithsunnah/bukhari/052.sbt.html (accessed September 28, 2005).

Chapter 14—Muhammad: Uncensored

1. Thanks to Johannes J. G. Jansen, author of *The Neglected Duty: The Creed of Sadat's Assassins and Islamic Resurgence in the Middle East* (New York: Macmillan Publishing Company, 1986), for astutely articulating this phenomenon in the introduction to his book.
2. Al-Tabari, *The History of the King and the Prophets,* 39 volumes.
3. *Sahih al-Bukhari* [The Correct Books of Bukhari], Volume 4, Book 52, Number 44, narrated Abu Huraira, http://www.usc.edu/dept/MSA/fundamentals/hadithsunnah/bukhari/052.sbt.html (accessed September 28, 2005).
4. *Sahih al-Bukhari* [The Correct Books of Bukhari], Volume 4, Book 52, Number 73, narrated 'Abdullah bin Abi Aufa, http://www.usc.edu/dept/MSA/fundamentals/hadithsunnah/bukhari/052.sbt.html (accessed September 28, 2005).
5. *Sahih al-Bukhari* [The Correct Books of Bukhari], Volume 4, Book 52, Number 258, narrated Ibn 'Umar, http://www.usc.edu/dept/MSA/fundamentals/hadithsunnah/bukhari/052.sbt.html (accessed September 28, 2005).
6. Qutb, *Milestones Along the Road,* 51–52.
7. *Sahih Muslim* [The Correct Books of Muslim], Book 017, Number 4206, http://www.usc.edu/dept/MSA/fundamentals/hadithsunnah/muslim/017.smt.html (accessed September 29, 2005).
8. *Sahih al-Bukhari* [The Correct Books of Bukhari], Volume 8, Book 81, Number 778, narrated 'Aisha, http://www.usc.edu/dept/MSA/fundamentals/hadithsunnah/bukhari/081.sbt.html (accessed September 29, 2005).
9. Ibn Kathir, *The Beginning and the End,* 569–660.
10. Ibn Hisham, *The Life of Muhammad,* 205, 299; Ibn Jarir, *The History of Messengers and Kings,* vol 3 (N.p.: n.d.), 251. See also *Sahih al-Bukhari* [The Correct Books of Bukhari], Volume 2, Book 14, Number 8; Volume 4, Book 52, Number 143; and *Ibn Ishaq in English* (N.p.: n.d.), 511.
11. Ibn Hisham, *The Life of Muhammad,* pt. 6, vol. 3, p. 8; author's translation.

Chapter 15—The Unrelenting Bloodbath

1. Zohdy, Maghed, and Zoummar, "The Second Inevitability for Confrontation," *Constitution of Al-Jihad,* in Ahmed, *The Armed Prophet.* To see the hadith from its primary source, go to the University of Southern California Web site and look up *Sahih Muslim* [The Correct Books of Muslim], Book 1, Number 29, http://www.usc

.edu/dept/MSA/fundamentals/hadithsunnah/muslim/001.smt.html (accessed September 29, 2005).

Chapter 16—Ibn Taymiyyah: Linking Muhammad to Modern Times

1. Encyclopedia Britannica Online, s.v. "Al-Hasan al-Basri," http://www.britannica.com/eb/article-9039442 (accessed September 29, 2005).
2. "Rabi`a al `Adawiyya," Sidi Muhammad Press, http://sufimaster.org/adawiyya.htm (accessed September 29, 2005).
3. Imam Abu Hamid al-Ghazzali, *Ihya Ulum ad-Din* [The Revival of the Signs of Religion] and Dr. Jemil Gezi, *Sufism: the Other Face* (Cairo: N.p., 1980).
4. "Shaykh al-Islaam Ibn Taymiyyah," Scholar's Biographies, fatwa-online.com, http://www.fatwa-online.com/scholarsbiographies/8thcentury/ibntaymiyyah.htm (accessed September 29, 2005).
5. Trevor Stanley, "Definition: Kufr - Kaffir - Takfir – Takfiri," Perspectives on World History and Current Events," http://www.pwhce.org/takfiri.html (accessed September 29, 2005).
6. Zohdy, Maghed, and Zoummar, "The Second Inevitability for Confrontation," *Constitution of Al-Jihad*, in Ahmed, *The Armed Prophet*.

Chapter 17—Calling Radicals to Cease-fire

1. Arabic Web site, http://murajaat.com/, author's translation (accessed July 2005).
2. For more information go to: http://www.tkb.org/Country.jsp?countryCd=EG. Under "Patterns of Global Terrorism," click on the "overview" for the year 1998.
3. Ibid. Click on the "overview" for the year 1999.
4. "A Matter of Time," *Al-Ahram Weekly* 597, August 1–7, 2002, http://weekly.ahram.org.eg/2002/597/eg5.htm (accessed August 31, 2005).
5. Jailan Halawi, "A New Page?," *Al-Ahram Weekly* 659, October 9–15, 2003, http://weekly.ahram.org.eg/print/2003/659/eg5.htm.
6. Arabic Web site, http://murajaat.com/, author's translation (accessed July 2005).
7. Jailan Halawi, "Time for a Historic Reconciliation?," *Al-Ahram Weekly* 592, June 27–July 3, 2002, http://weekly.ahram.org.eg/2002/592/eg4.htm (accessed September 1, 2005).
8. Franz Schurmann, "Can an Ex-Assassin Bring Peace to Egypt?" Pacific News Service, July 25, 2003, http://news.pacificnews.org/news/view_article.html?article_id=85b58beb91ae0736b9166b8924f986b6

(accessed September 29, 2005).

9. Halawi, "Time for a Historic Reconciliation?"
10. Ibid.
11. Kazuhiko Fujiwara, "Religious Enlightenment Could Contain Islamic Terrorism," *Daily Yomiui*, July 17, 2002, why-war.com, http://www.why-war.com/news/read.php?id=1902&printme (accessed September 29, 2005).
12. Saleh, "Egypt Hails Militants' Truce."
13. World Tribune.com, "Egypt Allows Prison Convention of Outlawed Radical Group," June 27, 2002, http://216.26.163.62/2002/me_egypt_06_27.html (accessed September 1, 2005).
14. Ibid.
15. Amir Taheri, "Islamic Extremists Recant," *New York Post,* October 10, 2003, as appearing on Benador Associates Web page, http://www.benadorassociates.com/article/609 (accessed September 29, 2005).
16. "Sadat Killing Mastermind Freed," BBC News UK edition, September 29, 2003, http://news.bbc.co.uk/1/hi/world/middle_east/3147598.stm (accessed September 1, 2005).
17. Zohdy, Maghed, and Zoummar, "The Road Is Made Clear," *Constitution of Al-Jihad*, in Ahmed, *The Armed Prophet.*
18. *The Last Hour* (in Arabic), February 20, 2002, http://www.akhbarelyom.org.eg/akhersaa/issues/3513/0501.html (author's translation).
19. Ibid.
20. *River of Memories* book summary, 2003, www.freemuslim.org/sohof/Truths/nahr%20zekriyatl.htm (in Arabic) (author's translation).
21. Ibid.

Chapter 18—The Quran for the Twenty-first Century

1. Fareed Zakaria, "How We Can Prevail," *Newsweek,* July 18, 2005, 38–41.
2. *Sahih al-Bukhari* [The Correct Books of Bukhari], Volume 9, Book 89, No. 252, narrated 'Abdullah bin 'Umar, http://www.usc.edu/dept/MSA/fundamentals/hadithsunnah/bukhari/089.sbt.html (accessed September 30, 2005).

Chapter 19—Take Religion Out of the Fight

1. CBSNews.com, "Falwell Sorry For Bashing Muhammad," October 14, 2002, http://www.cbsnews.com/stories/2002/10/11/60minutes/main525316.shtml (accessed July 28, 2005).
2. Jay Esteban, "Project ISLAM: Helping Philippine Muslims," *Christian*

World News, August 6, 2004, http://www.cbn.com/CBNNews/CWN/080604projectIslam.asp (accessed September 30, 2005).

Chapter 20—Engage the Silent Muslim Majority

1. See *Sahih al-Bukhari* [The Correct Books of Bukhari], Volume 9, Book 88, Number 219, narrated Abu Bakra, http://www.usc.edu/dept/MSA/fundamentals/hadithsunnah/bukhari/088.sbt.html (accessed September 30, 2005).

GLOSSARY

The glossary includes an informal pronunciation guide for words that are difficult to pronounce. The pronunciation guides are intended to improve ease of reading and do not reflect formal linguistic standards for phonetic spellings

A.H. "After *hijra*." The Islamic calendar starts in the year that Muhammad made the *hijra* from Mecca to Medina.

Abandoned Duty, The (1987) Written by Abdul Salam Faraj, this fiery booklet called Muslims to sacrifice themselves to fulfill the abandoned duty of jihad.

Adawiya, Rabi'a al- (d. A.H. 801) Muslim woman who proposed that Muslims should focus on the love of Allah, not the fear of Allah. This was a major philosophical step for Sufism.

Al-Azhar Oldest, largest, and most powerful Islamic university in the world based in Cairo, Egypt

Aristocrats, the Osama bin Laden and Ayman al-Zawahiri. In the late 1980s, these two leaders became prominent in radical Islam. Unlike their predecessors, they were men of privilege and means. After successfully pushing the Soviet Union out of Afghanistan, they turned their sites toward a new target and masterminded the attacks of 9/11.

Bakr, Abu [*AW-bu BAW-kir*] Close companion of Muhammad and first caliph after Muhammad's death

Banna, Hasan al- (1906–1949) He started out as an Arabic language teacher in elementary school in Egypt and ended up as the founder of the Muslim Brotherhood, the grandfather of all modern Muslim radical groups. His phenomenal organizational skills brought a half million members in Egypt alone by the mid-1940s. The pamphlets he wrote on various topics are widely available.

Basri, Al-Hasan al- (d. A.H. 110) Scholar of Sufism in the second century of Islam

caliph An Arabic word that means "leader." The term *caliph* specifically refers to the successors of Muhammad who served as the political and spiritual heads of Islam.

caliphate The "office or dominion" of the caliph. The last caliphate was based in Turkey until its fall in 1924.

Constitution of Al-Jihad Document written from prison by leaders of Al-Jihad and completed in 1986. It justifies the overthrow of the Egyptian government and gives a clear picture of the radical mind-set.

Evangelists, the Dr. Salah Sariah, Shokri Mustafa, and Abdul Salam Faraj. These men took the writings of the Founders to heart and gave their lives to put them into practice during the 1970s and 1980s. The life cycle of these writers was to become committed to radical Islam, found their own radical group, write a manifesto of their position, carry out an attack against the government, get captured, go on trial, and be executed. These writings are rarely available in English or analyzed in depth, but they are fueling the next generation of radicals.

Faraj, Abdul Salam (1954–1982) [*AB-dool suh-LAAM FAR-ahj*] Author of *The Abandoned Duty,* a fiery manuscript that argues for jihad as the only way to establish Islamic law and government. He was also one of the founding members of Al-Jihad, the military branch of Al-Gama'a al-Islamiyyah that assassinated Egyptian President Anwar Sadat. He was executed at the age of twenty-eight.

fitnah, al- a state of confusion

Five Pillars of Radical Islamic Philosophy The guiding principles of radical Muslims as determined by a content analysis of key writings by Islamic radicals (particularly Sayyid Qutb, Abdul Salam Faraj, Dr. Salah Sariah, and Al-Jihad leaders who wrote *Constitution of Al-Jihad*). These pillars are: 1. Obey no law but Islamic law. 2. Infidels are all around. 3. Islam must rule. 4. Jihad is the only way to win. 5. Faith is the reason.

Founders, the Hasan al-Banna, Abul ala Mawdudi, and Sayyid Qutb. These men were scholars of Islam, and through great organizational skills and deeply inspirational writings, they spread a return to Islamic fundamentalism starting in the late 1920s. Their call for jihad was clear but sophisticated. Many conservative Muslim Web sites make their writings available in Arabic, English, and other languages.

fundamentalism Christian fundamentalism emphasizes "the literally interpreted Bible as fundamental to Christian life and teaching." In the same way, Islamic fundamentalism emphasizes the literally interpreted Quran and sunnah as fundamental to Muslim life and teaching.

Gama'a al-Islamiyyah, Al- [*Al-je-MI-yuh al-is-luh-MEE-yuh*] Islamic radical group founded in Egypt at Cairo University in 1978. This group was behind the assassination of Egyptian President Anwar Sadat in 1981 and battled the Egyptian government for years until declaring a cease-fire in 1998.

hadith [*ha-DEETH*] The record of Muhammad's words and actions. This material was committed to memory for several generations and then collected and recorded by Muslim scholars. The most reliable collections were put together by al-Bukhari (A.H. 194–256) and Muslim (A.H. 202–261).

Hizb al-Tahrir Palestinian terrorist group. Dr. Salah Sariah formed an Egyptian branch in 1974. Groups by this name are still active in various places of the world.

ijma'ah [*EEJ-muh-yuh*] Means "a group in agreement." It refers to the practice in Islamic law whereby new law is established for situations not specifically covered in the Quran or sunnah.

Islam The religion founded by Muhammad. Its beliefs are based on the Quran and the life of Muhammad.

jahiliyyah An Islamic concept referring to the spiritual condition of pre-Islamic Arabian society. It is described as a state of ignorance of God's message. The term was popularized by Qutb, who used it to refer not only to non-Muslims but also to Muslims who failed to practice true Islam, in his opinion.

Jihad, Al- Also known as Islamic Jihad. Radical group founded in 1979 as the militant branch of Al-Gama'a al-Islamiyyah. It's leaders carried out the assassination of Egyptian President Anwar Sadat.

Kharijites [*Kuh-WARJ-ites*] The first significant Muslim extremist movement. The Kharijites assassinated the third successor of Muhammad.

Khattib, Umar ibn al- Second successor of Muhammad

Khomeini, Ayatollah (1957–) Leader of the Iranian revolution

Laden, Osama bin The leader of Al-Qaeda, bin Laden was born in 1957 in Saudi Arabia, the seventeenth son of a wealthy construction magnate. Bin Laden earned his reputation as a jihadist by fighting against the Russians in Afghanistan in the 1980s. In 1998 he declared a fatwa against the United States and has been masterminding missions against her ever since, most notably the 9/11 attacks.

Maghed, Assim Abdul One of the three authors of the *Constitution of Al-Jihad*

Mawdudi, Abul ala (1903–1979) [*AW-bool ah-la-mow-DOO-dee*] Born in India in 1903, he graduated from college with a bachelor's degree by the age of fifteen and left home to work as a newspaper editor. Mawdudi's prolific writing focused on reviving fundamentalist Islam, and he was instrumental in the creation of Pakistan with the intention of making it a Muslim state. His writings are widely available in Arabic, English, and other languages.

Message of Faith, The (1973) Written by Dr. Salah Sariah, it gave proof that Islamic society in general had fallen into apostasy.

Milestones Along the Road (1964) The seminal work by Sayyid

Qutb that provided the inspiration for the radical groups that came after him.

Muslim fundamentalist A Muslim who wants to practice Islam according to the original sources: the Quran and the life of the prophet Muhammad, just as a fundamentalist Christian calls for practicing Christianity according to the Bible and the life of Jesus.

Muslim radical A fundamentalist Muslim who practices all of the teachings of Quran and hadith, including jihad as a call to all Muslims to establish the worldwide caliphate and implement Islamic law. A radical Muslim may choose to practice jihad peacefully through teaching and persuasion, or he may decide that the most effective jihad will be through force and violence.

Muslim A person who practices Islam

Mustafa, Shokri (1942–1978) [*SHO-kree moo-STA-fuh*] Considered intolerant even among radicals, Mustafa founded al-Takfir wal-Hijra and called for his group to separate themselves from infidel society as they prepared to overthrow the secular leaders. Al-Qaeda followed this strategy by isolating and training its members in remote camps.

nasikh The principle of continuing revelation in the Quran. In the case of a contradiction, newer teachings abrogate, or cancel, older teachings.

Nasser, Gemal Abdul President of Egypt from 1956–1970. Nasser refused to implement Islamic law, causing radical groups to rebel against him. He took harsh measures against them.

Ottoman Empire Muslim caliphate lasting from 1301–1924 A.D.

Prisoners, the Abod Zoummar, Karam Zohdy, and Assim Abdul Maghed. This group is different from the evangelists because they were not executed for their attacks against the government. Instead, they were kept in prison, where they wrote two manuscripts defending their jihad against Egyptian authority in the 1980s.

Quran The words of Allah revealed to Muhammad in seventh-century Arabia. The Quran is 114 chapters long—about the length of the Christian New Testament.

Qutb, Sayyid (1906–1965) [*SAH-yeed KOO-tib*; OO as in foot] Born in Egypt, Qutb finished memorizing the Quran at the incredibly young age of ten and went on to work as an Arabic language teacher and a literary critic. Of all radical writings, his are the most widely read and circulated, particularly his book *Ma'alim fi'l Tariq* [Milestones Along the Road], for which he was executed by the Egyptian government in 1965.

Radical Muslim *See Muslim radical*

Rahman, Hamdi Abdul One of the top eight historic leaders of Al-Gama'a al-Islamiyyah. He helped write and print their new books justifying a cease-fire and calling for their group to work toward their goals without violence.

Rahman, Sheikh Omar Abdul (1938–) Spiritual leader of Al-Gama'a al-Islamiyyah in Egypt at the time of the assassination of President Anwar Sadat. He was convicted of masterminding the first bombing of the World Trade Centers in New York and is currently incarcerated in the United States.

Rightly guided caliphs Muslim caliphate lasting from A.H. 11–40/A.D. 632–661. The four rightly guided caliphs in order were Abu Bakr, Umar ibn Al-Khattib, Uthman bin Affan, and Ali ibn Abu Talib.

Sariah, Dr. Salah (1933–1975) [*suh-LA suh-REE-yuh*] Author of *The Message of Faith* (1973), which gave detailed arguments to prove that Muslim society in general had fallen into apostasy. His writing shows the faith-based mind-set of the Islamic radical.

sharia [*SHAH-ree-uh*] Islamic law based first on the Quran (revelation from Allah), then on sunnah (example of Muhammad), and finally on *ijma'ah* (the informed decision of a qualified group of Muslim scholars).

Sufism Islamic sect that was most popular during the time of Ibn

Taymiyyah. It focuses on the inner, personal life of Muslims and rejects jihad as a physical battle in favor of jihad as a battle within oneself to follow the teachings of Islam.

sunnah The words and actions of Muhammad, the prophet of Islam. The record of these words and actions are called hadith.

Taymiyyah, Ibn (1268–1328) [*ib-in tie-MEE-yuh*] A conservative Islamic scholar who is often quoted by radicals. He called for Muslims to fight jihad against the Mongols who had conquered the Islamic caliphate.

Umayyad Dynasty Muslim caliphate lasting from A.H. 41–132/ A.D. 661–751

Walid, Khalid ibn One of Muhammad's companions, known as the "Sword of Allah" for his fierceness in battle; a hero to modern radicals

Zarqawi, Abu Mussab al- (1966–) A Jordanian who is leading Al-Qaeda in Iraq. He is infamous for kidnapping and beheading westerners.

Zawahiri, Ayman al- (1951–) [*AY-man al-zaw-wuh-HEER-ee*] Second in command of Al-Qaeda. He was a leader in Al-Gama'a al-Islamiyyah in Egypt before joining forces with Osama bin Laden.

Zohdy, Karam (1952–) One of the three authors of *Constitution of Al-Jihad.* He was imprisoned from 1981 to 2003 for his role in the assassination of Sadat. He has acted as leader and spokesman for the cease-fire announced in 1997.

Zoummar, Abod One of the three authors of *Constitution of Al-Jihad.* Also wrote a key book in 1986 titled *Strategy of Al-Jihad.* He has been in prison since 1981, but in 2005 he put his name on the ballot for the presidential election, running on a fifty-point platform.

BIBLIOGRAPHY

Ahmed, Rifaat Sayed. *The Armed Prophet.* London: Riad El-Rayyes Books, 1991. (Arabic language)

Faraj, Abdul Salam. *The Abandoned Duty,* in Ahmed, *The Armed Prophet.* Translation into English by Habib Srouji.

Kathir, Ibn. *The Beginning and the End.* Beirut, Lebanon: The Revival of the Arabic Tradition Publishing House, 2001. (Arabic language)

———. *Quranic Commentary.* (Arabic language)

Kepel, Gilles. *Muslim Extremism in Egypt.* Berkeley and Los Angeles: University of California Press, 2003.

Mawdudi, Abul Ala. *Jihad in Islam.* Lahore, Pakistan: Islamic Publications. http://www.islamistwatch.org/texts/maududi/maududi.html.

Qutb, Sayyid. *Milestones Along the Road.* Delhi, India: Markazi Maktaba Islami.

Sahih al-Bukhari [The Correct Books of Bukhari]. English translation by Dr. Muhammad Muhasin Khan. Material was accessed at the University of Southern California Web site, 2005.

Sahih Muslim [The Correct Books of Muslim]. English translation by Abdul Hamid Siddiqui. Two recent publishers: Kitab Bhaven, New Delhi, India, 2000 and Kazi Publications in Chicago, IL, 1976. Material was accessed at the University of Southern California Web site, 2005.

Sariah, Dr. Salah. *The Message of Faith,* in Ahmed, *The Armed Prophet.* Translation into English by Habib Srouji.

Zohdy, Karam, Assim Abdul Maghed, and Abod Zoummar. *Constitution of Al-Jihad,* in Ahmed, *The Armed Prophet.* Translation into English by Habib Srouji.

Zoummar, Abod. *The Strategy of Al-Jihad,* in Ahmed, *The Armed Prophet.* Translation into English by Habib Srouji.

INDEX

N

O

P

Q

R

S

AUTHOR'S ACADEMIC CREDENTIALS

Dr. Gabriel's academic credentials in Islamic scholarship include:

- Bachelor's, master's, and doctorate degrees in Islamic History and Culture from Al-Azhar University, Cairo, Egypt

- Graduating second in his class of six thousand students for his bachelor's degree. This ranking was based on cumulative scores of oral and written exams given at the end of each school year.

- One of the youngest lecturers ever hired at Al-Azhar University. He started lecturing after he finished his master's degree and was working to finish his doctorate.

- Traveling lecturer. The university sent him to countries around the Middle East as a lecturer in Islamic history.

Al-Azhar University is the most respected, authoritative Islamic university in the world. It has been in continuous operation for more than one thousand years.

In addition to his academic training, Dr. Gabriel had practical experience, serving as the imam at a mosque in the Cairo suburbs.

After Dr. Gabriel became a Christian in 1993, he pursued a Christian education. His credentials in Christian education include:

- Discipleship Training School with Youth With A Mission in Cape Town, South Africa (1996)

- Master's degree in World Religion from Florida Christian University in Orlando, Florida (2001)

- Doctorate degree in Christian Education from Florida Christian University in Orlando, Florida (2002)

- Induction as a fellow in the Oxford Society of Scholars, September 2003

He knows. He speaks the truth. You need to listen.

We know that you have gained new insight by reading this book. Here are three other books by Mark Gabriel that you won't want to miss.

ISLAM and TERRORISM

What motivates a terrorist?
Islam has been veiled in a vast sea of misinformation for too long! Learn the truth.

$13.99 / 0-88419-884-7

ISLAM and the Jews

What fuels the conflict? There are powerful cultural and spiritual forces at work right now, and you have a role in the unfolding world events.

$13.99 / 0-88419-956-8

JESUS and Muhammad

What similarities did Jesus and Muhammad share? See how the leaders of the two largest religions in the world described themselves, defined God, recruited their followers, and more.

$13.99 / 1-59185-291-9

5596

"America needs to wake up...soon!"

Visit your local bookstore
Call 800-599-5750 www.frontlineissues.com
Mention Offer: BP6104

FRONT LINE
A STRANG COMPANY